Message
on the
Wall

A Diane Production
2022

Other Books
By
Diane Browne

5 Paranormal Tales

5 More Paranormal Tales

5 Tudor Tales

Victor's Place

Message on the Wall

20 Myths, Mysteries, Legends & Hauntings

Diane Browne

Print December 2022
ISBN 979-8362476335
Book cover design © 2022 Diane Browne.
Author's email paranormalx2000@hotmail,com
Author's website Paranormal X www.paranornalx.yolasite.com

DEDICATION

To
My Two Legends
Maverick & Tobias

and also

Mark Wojtszek
for giving me the opportunity to have fun gathering and
researching the stories.

.

CONTENTS

INTRODUCTION

Message on the Wall came about as short audio segments when I was asked by Mark Wojtaszek to make paranormal-themed fillers for his internet radio show. I didn't have a title when I produced the first about a sea captain who found messages scrawled on a cabin wall aboard his ship giving directions to change course. I called it Message on the Wall, and that is how Mark introduced the segment. From then on that is what it was called. I made the audio introduction, "And now it's time for" (deepening my voice) "Message on the Wall." I can't say how many times someone as said in a deep voice, "Message on the Wall." It always makes me smile seeing how I used the computer to deepen the tone.

Some of the segments were too long for Mark but they can all be found, along with "Haunted Cemeteries" at my Youtube channel, SnowyOwl2000.

The stories I have put together here are new stories along with a couple from the fillers. To put all the information found during my research would make a series of books. If any of the stories take your interest, there are plenty of websites and books in the reference section.

Thank You to Mark Wojtaszek.

Enjoy!

AL CAPONE

Al Capone

Al Capone is one of the most well-known criminals of the prohibition era. Alphonse Gabriel Capone was born in Brooklyn, New York, on January 17, 1899, being the fourth child of Gabriel and Theresa Capone. From nine surviving children, only one, the last was a girl born in 1912. Gabriel Capone died in 1920, leaving his widow to raise three children of school age.

Al was a promising student, though he didn't like following the rules. He was expelled at fourteen after a teacher hit him and he hit her back. From there, he found odd jobs and with his love of baseball, played for a team when he was seventeen. Then Al came under the influence of Johnny Torrio, a well-dressed Italian-born mobster.

He was working as a doorman at a Coney Island club when he insulted a female patron and in response was slashed with a knife on the left side of his face. The knife-wielding man was the girl's brother. This incident led to his most hated nickname, "Scarface," often saying it was a war wound. Being a snappy dresser, his friends called him "Snorky," meaning well dressed. Al often appeared in the sports pages attending baseball games and boxing matches, claiming to be a promoter.

When Torrio moved to Chicago to work for Big Jim Colosimo, Capone went with him. By this time, he had married Mae Coughlin, a month after their only child, Albert Francis Capone was born. Nicknamed Sonny, in 1966, he dropped his last name to get away from the Capone fame. He didn't follow his father and uncles into a life of crime and after three marriages producing four daughters, he died in 2004.

When Big Jim Colosimo was murdered, Al was the main suspect with the death improving his position in the gang's ranks. If this was the case, it would have been carried out on the orders of Torrio, who became boss of the South Side Chicago outfit. The gang soon began bootlegging, something Colosimo had no interest in. With Torrio becoming boss, Al Capone became heir to Torrio's empire. Torrio was the main instigator in carving out the Chicago territories. There was more money than ever to be made with the ban on alcohol, but more always wants more. Dean O'Banion, boss of the North Side, encouraged speakeasies to relocate to his turf. He then stole a shipment belonging to the Genna Crime Family and even worse, double-crossed Torrio, which inevitably led to a turf war beginning with O'Bannion's death.

Several attempts were made on Al Capone's life but when Johnny Torrio survived a drive-by shooting, he quickly got the message. Deciding to retire, he handed control over to 26-year-old Al Capone, making him one of the youngest crime bosses.

Basing himself in Cicero, 8-miles outside of Chicago, a famous assassination attempt took place on September 20, 1926. Several cars passed by the restaurant to the Hawthorne, a hotel where Al Capone was dining. Suddenly, there was a blaze of bullets, and everyone hit the floor. At its end, there was no damage because they were blanks. Then a second convoy passed. This time, real bullets shattered the windows, lodging into walls inside and out. It was all for nothing as only two people received minor injuries, a female guest and one of Capone's men. The Hawthorne remained a mob hangout up to 1970 when the place burnt down. Al Capone wasn't like Johnny Torrio and instead of being frightened off, got revenge.

There were drive-by shootings spilling out hundreds of bullets, with the public having the attitude that it didn't matter while they were killing each other. That all changed on St. Valentine's Day 1929.

At the time Al Capone was at his Florida home, which he had bought the year before in his wife's name. The main target was

George "Bugs" Moran, who became boss on the demise of Dean O'Banion, leaving a lot of old scores to settle. Moran was going to meet his crew that morning at a warehouse he rented on North Clark Street where they allegedly were waiting for a shipment of hijacked whiskey belonging to Capone. It was another hit that went wrong. Moran was running late and turning the corner, saw the police pull up outside the warehouse and, thinking it was a raid, walked away.

Men dressed as Chicago police officers and two plainclothes men that could have been taken for prohibition agents entered the building. Removing the weapons of all the men present, they were ordered to line up facing a wall. Albert Kachellek, Albert Weinshank, brothers Frank and Peter Gusenberg and Adam Heyer would have expected to be tipped off if a raid was due but weren't suspicious enough not to follow orders. Two other men, Reinhardt Schwimmer who just liked to hang out with gangsters, and John May, a mechanic working on a vehicle, were also lined up. With the men's backs turned to them, 70 rounds of bullets splattered across the wall. The police officers were then seen taking the suited men away at gunpoint.

When the real police. arrived, they found all the men dead except Frank Gusenberg, who had been shot 14 times. Keeping to the code of silence or simply not knowing who the men were, he refused to say anything other than "yes" when asked if the killers wore police uniforms. He died a few hours later.

Bugs Moran had many enemies but pointed the finger at Al Capone, and the newspapers followed suit. At that time, Capone was at least well respected by the citizens of Chicago. He opened soup kitchens during the depression, serving three meals a day to the unemployed, but his good standing soon eroded. It was all well and good for gang members to kill one another, but this was unarmed hoodlums and two innocent men. John May's German shepherd dog "Highball" was the eighth victim. He was found cowering under a truck howling and trembling in fear. The dog was so traumatized it was felt best to put him down.

Investigators found that a landlady across the road from Moran's base had rented a room overlooking the street to two men. She and other witnesses identified mugshots of members of the Purple Gang but, as usual, recanted. The Jewish gang was later suspected of being involved in the kidnapping of Charles Lindbergh's 20-month-old son in 1932 as they often resorted to armed robbery and kidnapping, as well as being hitmen for hire.

Al Capone always denied having any involvement in the deaths, and yet it was a short time later that he began to see the ghost of Albert Kachellek. He often used the name James Clark, being better known as Jimmy.

After a meeting in Philadelphia with other crime family bosses headed by Charles "Lucky" Luciano, Al Capone and his bodyguard Frank Rio paid a visit to the Stanley Theater where it was arranged that Capone would be arrested for carrying a concealed weapon. Capone and Rio were sentenced to one year in prison but only served 10-months. For Capone, the Eastern State Penitentiary wasn't exactly what prison was meant to be. Al installed his own furniture rather than prison issue, which wasn't unusual for wealthier prisoners who could afford it. He also had a ghost for a cellmate. It was here that

Al Capone. May 16, 1929. Pennsylvania Department of Corrections/FBI.

he would shout and yell at "Jimmy" to let him alone. After leaving prison, the St. Valentine's Day Massacre, as dubbed by the press, hadn't died down, and Jimmy didn't stay behind bars, continuing to haunt Capone, presumably to his dying day.

Al returned to his headquarters at the Lexington Hotel in Chicago, where he rented a whole floor, including rooms above and below for his bodyguards. Even here, he would wake in the night, making his men think there was an intruder. This was later put down to Capone having contracted syphilis shortly after moving to Chicago. No cure was known at that time but being treated in the early stages would have helped. Either out of embarrassment or denial, he didn't seek any treatment. Syphilis is a disease that causes sores and rashes, which then disappear from sight as it works its way into the organs of the body, including the brain. If Jimmy Clark was an hallucination, his valet, bodyguards, prisoners and prison officers at the Eastern State Penitentiary and Alcatraz must have fed into it with many claiming to have seen and heard the ghost.

Did Al Capone put out the hit on St. Valentine's Day, or did a vengeful Jimmy Clark think he did! That is something we will never know. There is plenty of evidence to say that it was set up by Capone, but that doesn't make it so. It's hard to believe that he would hire people so sloppy to leave such evidence for the police to find. The car they used was left a 10-minute drive from the murder site. In fact, attention was drawn to it when it was set on fire with an acetylene torch inside a garage after being partially dismantled. It would have been easier and quicker to do a respray and take it to a junkyard. Later that year, as part of a large cache, the guns used were found at the home of Fred "Killer" Burke, an associate of Al Capone. One would think such weapons would have been disposed of in some river after being used in such a high-profile crime, especially as ballistic tests found they had also been used in the murder of the Brooklyn mob boss, Frankie Yale on July 1, 1928. If someone was setting Al Capone up, it wouldn't be the first time.

Al Capone is known for being a gangster but is just as well known for being given the highest sentence for tax evasion. There is no doubt that he had bad defense lawyers who should have had some of the counts thrown out as the time limit had elapsed. Al was also under the assumption that you can't pay taxes on illegal earnings such as bootlegging, gambling and prostitution, but that was fixed with a court case in 1927 (United States v Sullivan). A deal fell through with the prosecution where Capone agreed to plead guilty in exchange for a two-year prison sentence, as the judge refused to agree to the terms. The trial began on October 5, 1931, when Judge Wilkerson exchanged the jury from another courtroom after being told potential jurors had been bribed. Once they were settled, 23 charges for tax evasion were levied at Al Capone, and the prosecution called their first witness. Charles Arndt, a U.S Tax Collector gave evidence that Al Capone hadn't paid any taxes between 1924 and 1929. A stream of witnesses were questioned about Capone's lifestyle, including purchasing his house on Palm Island in Florida. It hit the jury hard when they learned Capone paid his bills in cash of $100 and $500 notes while they struggled through the depression. Taking only a day for the prosecutors to rest their case, Capone's defense attempted to convince the jury that he was addicted to gambling, losing more on horse races than any he made from businesses he was involved in. Though gambling losses aren't tax-deductible, they presented bookies who claimed that Capone was consistent in losing. After 13-days of listening to the evidence, mainly hearsay and speculation, the jury left the courtroom to deliberate. It took them 8-hours to return a verdict of guilty for tax evasion on 3 of the 23 counts. It was another six days before the court convened and Judge Wilkerson, doing the bidding of the White House, put Al Capone away for the maximum 11 years. Many felt the sentence was also for crimes they couldn't get Capone on, especially the St. Valentine's Day Massacre.

Capone was taken to Atlanta where his prison cell was a home from home, along with Jimmy Clark. The rumor soon spread that Capone was living a life of luxury as he conducted business from prison. To make things more uncomfortable, in August 1934, he was transferred to the already infamous Alcatraz. Going from a fortress to a military prison, by the time Al got there, it had been modernized and intended to house the habitual violent criminals and continual troublemakers. Only having been in prison once before, Capone was a model prisoner and continued to be so. Even at Alcatraz, prison officers claimed to hear Capone shouting and having conversations with Jimmy Clark.

He joined the prison band named the Rock Islanders' playing the banjo every Sunday to the prisoners. He loved opera and the new craze of jazz, hiring artists for his speakeasies who became big-name celebrities. He even wrote his own songs, including "Madonna Mia" at Alcatraz.

Capone spent a lot of time in the prison hospital where he was first diagnosed with syphilis. In January 1939, he was transferred to Terminal Island in San Francisco. Having been a model prisoner at Alcatraz, his demeanor changed, becoming involved in many fights leading to bouts in solitary confinement and loss of privileges. According to his great-niece, Deirdre Capone, in treating his syphilis, he was injected with mercury. During his time at Terminal Island, he claimed he had been poisoned more than once in Alcatraz by other prisoners and a doctor.

After appeals from his wife, Capone was paroled in November 1939. He didn't go straight home but became a patient at the Union Memorial Hospital in Baltimore. He was one of the first people in America to be treated with penicillin. Unfortunately, this was too late to be the cure it is today.

The closeness of the Capone family could be seen as they rented a house in Baltimore and spent time with him at the hospital. After spending some time at the rented home to recover, they took a trip to New York before going to the Palm Island home. By this time Al was diagnosed as having the mental capacity of a 12-year-old.

Despite all he had been through in prison, including being stabbed by violent killer James Lucas, Capone lived for seven years after his release. He died at his Florida mansion on January 22, 1947, having had a stroke the day before.

Al Capone is just as active in death. Apart from haunting his Miami home, he still finds time to visit one of his favorite drinking places, The Green Mill Cocktail Lounge on N. Broadway Avenue, Chicago. Maybe it's because it remains exactly the same as when he was a patron. People claim to have seen Al in his usual booth or making a quick exit by the back door.

The Congress Plaza Hotel claims to be one of Chicago's most haunted hotels. During its heyday, card games in one of the meeting rooms took place every Friday with Capone being a regular, even to this day.

And there is, of course, Alcatraz, where banjo music is often heard in what was the shower room where Al would practice away from the other prisoners.

ASSASSINATION & CURSE OF ABRAHAM LINCOLN

Abraham Lincoln Presidential Portrait from Pixabay

Growing up, Abraham Lincoln was more interested in books than farm work that his family accused him of being lazy. However, his self-education led to him becoming a lawyer and, inevitably, politics. Lincoln became the 16th President on November 6, 1860, with 40% of the popular vote. Being dubbed "Honest Abe" he was "Unpopular Abe" in the south, receiving zero votes from 10 out of the 15 southern states. If it had been a two-horse race rather than four competing parties, it could have been a different outcome. Instead, the split votes between Democratic Stephen A. Douglas, Constitutional Union John Bell and Southern Democratic John C Breckinridge allowed Lincoln to slip into the White House.

Despite the unrest, Abraham Lincoln didn't believe there would be an inevitable Civil War that began seventeen months into his presidency. He couldn't envisage the southern states carrying out their threat to break away from the union, but they weren't bluffing. South Carolina took the lead with others quickly following to become the Confederate States of America before the Lincoln's moved into the White House.

Lincoln's reelection success looks much better on paper, gaining just over 55% of the popular vote against George B McClellan for the Democratic Party. However, it should be remembered that the Confederate States no longer had a vote.

The Lincoln's moved into the White House in March 1861 with their two sons, Thomas "Tad" and William "Willie," who died at the White House on February 20, 1862 from typhoid fever. The eldest, Robert, was at Harvard, and their second son Eddie had passed away 11 years previous.

Abraham Lincoln's dream is an often-related tale that goes into the realms of an urban legend, as it was first told 20 years after his death. Ward Hill Lamon worked the law circuit with Lincoln, being a friend and sometimes bodyguard. Lamon claimed to be among a group of guests when the president related a dream he had a few nights before. This wouldn't be unusual as Lincoln showed an interest in dreams and their meanings. In the dream, Lincoln awoke to the sound of sobbing. Going in search of what or who was making the sound, on entering the East Room, he saw a casket draped with a flag. Soldiers were on guard, and a group of people stood weeping. Asking who had died, one of the guards replied, "the president."

On April 14, 1865, the Lincoln's were scheduled to attend the comedy "Our American Cousin" at Ford's Theater. Mary was still mourning the loss of her son and claimed to have a headache. Abraham would have cancelled except that his guest, General Ulysses Grant, had changed his plans, visiting family in New Jersey instead. It was also published in the Evening Star newspaper that the president and General Grant would be attending. At the last minute, Lincoln invited Major Henry Rathbone and his fiancée Clara Harris. Arriving late, the play was stopped while the Lincolns and their guests were seated in a private box.

During the third act, the Lincoln's moved closer together and holding hands, Mary asked, "What will Miss Harris think of me hanging on to you so?" Abraham replied. "She won't think anything about it." Those are the last words he spoke.

While the audience was watching the play, a plot was put into action. The original intention was to kidnap Abraham Lincoln with a president being worth a lot more than a general when using him for a prisoner exchange. It was changed by John Wilkes Booth from kidnapping to murder only hours before. And not just the president was meant to die that night as it was to be a series of assassinations.

John Wilkes Booth (26), a celebrated actor, would kill President Lincoln and General Grant in the theater he knew so well. Lewis Powell (20), a confederate soldier and David Herold (22), a pharmacist assistant, was sent to murder the Secretary of State, William H Seward. The last on the list was Vice President Andrew Johnson. Booth sent George Atzerodt (29), a confederate sympathizer to do the job.

Top left George Atzerodt.
Top middle Lewis Powell.
Top right John Wilkes Booth.
Bottom David Herold.
Al photographs Alexander Gardner – Library of Congress's Prints and Photographs.

Around 10pm, Booth entered the back of the theater. Being well known, his presence wasn't questioned when he asked Edward Spangler to hold his horse. Booth was confident enough to be only armed with a small one bullet gun and a dagger.

Whether providence or planned, Lincoln's bodyguard, John Parker, should have been guarding the door to the private theater box but instead left his post to watch the play. During the intermission, he went to a nearby saloon and didn't return. Curiously, Booth spent some time at the same saloon and no doubt would have seen John Parker.

It would be reasonable to think that Parker would at least be demoted. Instead, he was assigned to be a bodyguard to Mary Lincoln, who dismissed him after accusing him of helping to murder the president. Parker joined the DC police department when it was formed in 1861 and managed to hold onto the job despite being found drunk on duty several times, as well as visiting a brothel. His luck ran out in 1868 when he was caught sleeping on duty one time too many. He died in 1890 at 60-years-old and is buried in an unmarked grave.

With the entrance left unguarded, John Wilkes Booth entered the theater box. Knowing the play, he waited until everyone would be laughing, helping to cover the sound of the gunshot. Placing the nozzle of the Derringer around 5-inches away from the president, he couldn't miss as he shot him in the back of the head. There must have been some disappointment as the bullet was probably meant for General Grant. And amazingly, the president was still alive.

Major Henry Rathbone reacted to the shot and grabbed Booth, who used the dagger to stab him in the shoulder before jumping from the box onto the stage. Rathbone escorted Mary Lincoln from the theater before passing out from loss of blood.

Fortunately, or maybe, unfortunately, he survived to marry Clara two years later with the couple having three children. He continued to live with the guilt at not saving the president and was only 33-years-old in 1870 when he resigned from the army. Finding it difficult to hold down a job, he began to have violent outbursts, accusing Clara of having an affair and resenting the attention she paid to the children. On December 23, 1883, Rathbone shot and stabbed his wife to death. He was arrested and charged with the murder but declared insane, so didn't stand trial and was placed in an asylum where he died 27 years later. The three children Henry (13), Gerald (12) and Clara (11), were cared for by Clara's brother.

Once the conspirators completed their mission, they were to meet up and make for the boarding house of sympathizer, Mary Surratt. For all the planning, Booth and Herold met on route. Somewhere along the way, Booth broke his leg, either when he jumped onto the stage or by being thrown from his horse as it stumbled and fell on top of him. The two men visited Doctor Mudd who knew Booth well. Giving them time to get away, Mudd waited until the next day before he reported treating Booth's broken leg.

The delay cost Mudd his freedom. He was charged with conspiracy and sentenced to life in prison. In March 1869, Doctor Mudd was set free with a pardon from President Andrew Jackson, though the conviction still stands. Samuel Mudd had been seen in the company of three of the main conspirators but denied meeting Booth, which leaves some historians to believe that Mudd was in on the plot to at least kidnap Lincoln. His name became synonymous with the phrase, "Your name is Mud," to disparage someone. He was 49 years old when he died on January 10, 1883.

A unit of soldiers tracked Booth to a farmer's barn in Virginia. Herold gave himself up while soldiers set fire to the barn in an attempt to smoke Booth out. Sergeant Boston Corbett looked through a gap into the barn and, seeing Booth, shot him almost in the same place as Lincoln. Booth was dragged to the farmhouse where he lingered for several hours before dying.

From there, it depends on which version is to be believed. The body was taken back to Washington, and Corbett was court-martialed for killing Booth as the order was to take him alive. By this time, unionists saw Corbett as a hero and he was released to a cheering crowd. He was discharged from the army in August 1865 and became a preacher.

Years later, a man claimed to be John Wilkes Booth with a story that the man in the barn had been mistaken for him.

David Herold was sent with Lewis Powell to hold his horse while he completed his mission. He was then meant to guide Powell out of Washington. The Secretary of State was recuperating at his Lafayette Park home after a coach accident in which he had broken his arm and jaw.

Just after 10pm, Powell, carrying a gun and dagger supplied by Booth, knocked on the door to the Seward home. Giving the excuse that he had medicine from the doctor instantly caused suspicion as the doctor had left only half an hour earlier. With the butler not allowing Powell entry, he forced himself inside. Making his way upstairs, Powell was confronted by the son, Frederick Seward. Having a violent temper, Powell placed the gun against Frederick's head, but it misfired and so used it as a cudgel. The servant, William Bell, raced from the house to raise the alarm, putting the waiting Herold into a panic. Leaving Powell's horse, he fled the scene.

Now with just a dagger, Powell made it to William Seward's bedroom where he leapt on top of him, slashing at his face and neck. He then made his getaway, leaving behind an injured Frederick, his sister Fanny, brother Augustus, Sergeant George Robinson acting as guard and nurse, and finally Emerick Hansell, a messenger staying at the house. All survived, including William Seward due to him wearing a neck brace but the attack took its toll on his wife, Frances who died two months later.

Finding that he had been abandoned by Herold, Powell rode through the unfamiliar streets of Washington until his horse gave out and then went on foot. His timing was unfortunate as he arrived in bloodstained clothes at the Surratt boarding house where the police were in the process of arresting Mary Surratt and two of her boarders. She was found guilty of conspiracy in allowing the men to use her saloon and boarding house for their meetings.

The assassination of Vice President Andrew Jackson was supposed to take place at 10pm that night. Armed with a gun and dagger, George Atzerodt was recruited to kidnap Lincoln and was no murderer. Andrew Jackson was staying at the Kirkwood Hotel, and Atzerodt took a room on the floor above. He then went to the Kirkwood's bar, where he drank the night away before leaving Washington.

Atzerodt was arrested after he was seen dropping the dagger in his drunken state. He was publicly hanged on July 7, 1865, alongside David Herold, Lewis Powell and Mary Surratt

Anyone with links to John Wilkes Booth was picked up and placed in cells, including the owner of Ford's Theater, John T Ford and his two brothers. All were later released, but the government seized the theater. Edward Spangler was found guilty of holding the horse for Booth to escape and received a 6-year prison sentence.

The theater was closed and used as a warehouse. In 1893 restoration work caused a supporting pillar to collapse, bringing down three floors, killing 22 and injuring around 70 others that it was thought the theater was cursed. In 1933 it became the property of the National Park Service, and in 1968, having been restored, opened with a gala performance, though the president's box is always vacant.

Across the road from the Theater is the Peterson House which is now a museum. After the shooting, Abraham fell unconscious, having what witnesses described as a relaxed expression after the worries of the past four years. Deciding the Theater wasn't a suitable place, his prone body was taken outside. A boarder at the Peterson House waved them to go inside, and Lincoln was placed on a bed in a back room. Mary Lincoln was so distraught that she was sent to another room while her husband lay dying. Abraham Lincoln remained there with people coming and going up to his death at 7.22am, on April 15, 1865. Having had his clothing removed, he was wrapped in a flag, placed in a plain coffin, and transported to the White House to lay in state in the East Room.

Anna and William Petersen were German immigrants who had the house built. They lived in the upper rooms while renting out the lower. When the president was installed in the house Anna was away, and William was at his workshop, working late as usual sewing clothes. The assassination was a curse that touched the Peterson's who soon found their home, inside and out, a place of curiosity. Some didn't just want to look as souvenirs were grabbed, taking bricks from the building to cutting pieces out of the carpet and stripping wallpaper. Lincoln's deathbed can now be found at the Chicago History Museum.

Becoming a tourist attraction, it was a nuisance for the boarders who quickly left. The war came to an end, leaving William with less work as he made army uniforms. He closed his business and went to work for another firm. Suffering from depression, the day after his 61st birthday, William took a nighttime walk. Sitting on a park bench, he removed a bottle from his coat pocket and took a good long drink. The bottle contained laudanum. Present family members say that William mistook the bottle for liquor that had been in his other pocket. A police officer found him and having his stomach pumped it was to no avail, dying on June 18, 1871. Anna followed her husband four months later with no record of how she died.

Mary Lincoln received an outpouring of sympathy and letters of condolence from around the world. She did her best to reply to all, especially Queen Victoria, knowing she would understand her loss with her beloved Prince Albert dying four years earlier. And like Queen Victoria, Mary was no stranger to spiritualism. She had hosted seances in the Red Room at the White House, some of which Abraham attended in the hope of receiving messages from their son Willie. Mary claimed that Willie would stand at the bottom of her bed, sometimes with his brother, Eddie.

It was not long after the death of Abraham Lincoln that rumors of him haunting the White House began.

Five years after the assassination, Mary, under an assumed name, visited William Mumler, who claimed to take photos of spirits. Though his reputation was sullied by a court case, Mary was photographed by Mumler. This resulted in a picture of her seated in a chair with the faint image of her husband placing his hands on her shoulders. It was made public with Mumler claiming that he didn't know the lady was Lincoln's widow, which proved to be fraudulent.

Mary Lincoln with ghost of Abraham Lincoln. Faked photograph by William H. Mumler.

Lincoln's ghost continues to wander the White House to this day, appearing in his bedroom which in his lifetime was his study, and also the Yellow Oval Room. Many notable people have claimed to have seen Lincoln, from a queen to British Prime Minister Winston Churchill.

THE BELL WITCH

Bell log cabin relocated beside the Bell School, Adams, Tennessee copyright Brian Stansberry 2016.

Receiving its name from the family it persecuted for over three years, The Bell Witch is an old story kept alive by books and movies.

It would probably have remained a local tale of a family being hexed by a neighbor or targeted by the devil if one of the sons hadn't allegedly kept a record of events.

The head of the family, John Bell, was born in 1760 in North Carolina. Having taken up an apprenticeship as a barrel maker, he later turned to farming. He married late in life at 32-years-old to 14-year-old Lucy Williams. John Bell was successful until 1801 when his crops failed. That was followed by two more bad years, leading John to uproot his growing family and move to Red River in Tennessee.

Beginning their dangerous journey during the winter of 1804, accompanied by a slave, John, Lucy and their five children aged between 14 and 1-year-old made their way to more fertile land. John bought a small acreage, less than half the size they left back in North

Carolina. He built a house for his still growing family with Elizabeth, known as Betsy, born in 1806, Richard in 1811 and the last, Joel in 1813.

The Bell family attended the Baptist Red River Church, and though they were far from rich at the side of some of their neighbors, they didn't want for anything. John became a prominent figure, an elder at the church and a deacon.

What became known as "The Family Troubles" began in 1817. John Bell was checking his crops when suddenly, between a row of corn, he saw a strange creature that he described as having the body of a dog and a head more like a rabbit. Being a typical American, he took several shots, only for the animal to vanish.

After John's encounter, his son Drewry saw an unusually large black bird on the property. Taking a shot, it also disappeared before his eyes.

The same evening after John's encounter, sounds were heard outside the cabin, likened to the beating of birds wings. Going outside to investigate, nothing could be seen. From then on, the sounds continued. Each night, John Bell and his sons would try to catch the culprit or culprits but to no avail. Things got worse when the phenomena moved inside the house. Stones fell from the ceiling to hit the unwary, furniture moved of its own accord, and there was the sound of chains being dragged across the floor. The three youngest children born in the house bore the brunt of the abuse that followed, but none more so than Betsy.

The children were kept awake at night by what they thought were rats gnawing on the bedposts, but there was no sign of damage or any rats. The phenomena increased when the bed covers were pulled off by unseen hands. Joel (3), Richard (7) and Betsy (11) would be slapped, pinched, and have their hair pulled, that Betsy always had bruises and welts.

A voice then followed, heckling John Bell up to the day he died.

When the family turned to the Bible, the voice mockingly recited scriptures. It claimed to be a witch who had been buried in the woods on the property. Her grave being disturbed, she was searching for her tooth that she said was under the house. If that was the case, she waited some time as the Bells had lived there 13-years.

Around a year before the troubles began, in July 1816, John Bell was in dispute with Benjamin Batts who sold him a slave but didn't hand the girl over for several days. Even though the sale had gone through, Batts wanted more money. Eventually, John sold the slave back to Batts with a 20% profit. Even today, some believe that Batts wanted revenge. John Bell. also thought that Batts wanted to see the family suffer in other ways by seeking out a neighboring relative, Kate Batts. Not only was Kate related to Benjamin Batts by marriage, but Lucy Bell was her aunt.

Kate Batts was hardworking, poor, and eccentric, making her an outcast. Kate also came out with words unbecoming of a lady that today could well be diagnosed as Tourette's. Maybe to make light of their tormentor, the Bell's called the witch Kate, to which the voice readily answered.

The three Bell slaves also came under the scrutiny of Kate, who would often beat them and wouldn't allow them to enter the house. One slave, Dean, who had moved to Red River with the family was the most vocal about his experiences, some being beyond belief. He claimed that a large, black two-headed dog would follow him. One day he was turned into a donkey and attacked by the dog, but this sounds better than being beaten by a farmer when John Bell hired his slave out.

Betsy suffered so much stress that she began having fainting spells and would be found semi-conscious after feelings of being suffocated. Theories have been raised that Betsy was the center of all the incidents, causing or hoaxing the phenomena. It's also been suggested that John Bell was visiting his daughter's bed at night, causing her stress and anxiety that followed Betsy to the grave. The skeptics can only blame the children for the voice from Betsy to her younger brother Richard.

The Bell's kept their troubles within the family for a year but eventually told a close friend what was happening. James Johnston was the first person outside the house that encountered what he eventually decided was an evil spirit. At first thinking it was no more than a practical joke being played by the children, it wasn't until he stayed the night that he changed his mind.

James' 34-year-old son, John, took great interest in the spirit and often helped the family by spending the night engaged in conversation with Kate, giving the Bell's a chance to sleep. However, Kate wasn't confined to the Bell house, and during a visit to the home of his brother, Calvin, the voice threatened to kill John Johnston.

Things didn't get any better when Benjamin Batts took his accusation that John Bell had cheated him over the sale of the slave to the church that held trials and investigations to resolve disputes between church members. John Bell was found to have acted in good faith, but not being satisfied with the decision, Batts took Bell to court where he was found guilty. This led the church to reopen the case. Being found guilty in a court of law caused embarrassment to the church and in January 1818, John Bell was excommunicated, meaning he was thrown out of the congregation. Some think the family troubles were also taken into account, which by then was common knowledge that the family was being plagued by an evil spirit.

John Bell petitioned the church several times but was refused readmission. He didn't get to see Benjamin Batts' excommunication in 1825 when he was found guilty of theft.

The poltergeist type activity took its toll on John Bell. He was slapped and punched by unseen hands and his shoes were pulled from his feet and thrown across the room. He had little sleep as the voice of Kate taunted and cursed him, making it clear that she would be present until he entered his grave.

John began to tire quickly. He had persistent migraine headaches and began to develop facial twitches. He complained of numbness and a tingling sensation until he eventually took to his bed. John Jr. cared for his father up to his death. Knowing there were three vials of medicine, when John Jr. went to the cupboard, there was only one containing a brown liquid. Kate set up gleefully, saying she had given the medicine to Old Jack while he slept and that had fixed him. John Jr. gave the liquid to a cat which died. Wanting to be rid of the poison or evidence, he threw it into the fire where it gave off a blue flame.

Over the years to the present day, John Bell's illness has been scrutinized, looking at it being a naturally occurring disease to murder. A low dose of arsenic over a period of time and a larger dose to kill him, would find many symptoms John Bell suffered. Betsy also had signs of a low dose of arsenic poisoning, which also causes respiratory problems.

After falling into a coma, John Bell died the next day on December 20, 1820. With so many hearing stories of the Bell Witch, John Bell's funeral was one of the largest in the county. It's said that as the grave was being filled in, Kate sang bawdy songs.

But Kate wasn't finished. When Betsy became engaged to her childhood sweetheart, Joshua Gardner, Kate made it quite clear that she disapproved of the match. They couldn't go anywhere together without the voice heckling them. Betsy eventually heeded the warning that if she married Joshua, she would not be happy, taking it to mean he would die like her father. She was truly in love with Joshua and held out until April 23, 1821, when she broke off the engagement, giving him up to save his life.

That was the last time Betsy and Joshua saw one another as he moved to the next county some 80 miles away. It was eight years before he married Sarah Donelson and had two children. Being a successful farmer and magistrate, he died in 1887.

Betsy married Richard Powell on March 21, 1824. Being 11-years older, he had been her teacher, and had also put pressure on Betsy not to marry Joshua, maybe even putting it into her mind that he would die if she married him. Some theorize that Powell was the Bell Witch as he may have rented a room at the Bell house when he first arrived to take up the teacher's position around 1815. There were also rumors that he took part in the dark arts. Though Betsy claimed the marriage of over 23 years was a happy one, Powell gave up teaching to go into politics. This came to an end in 1837 when he had a stroke. Betsy nursed him, but with no money coming in, they soon became destitute. Richard Powell died in January 1848, 11-years after his stroke.

After her husband's death, Lucy remained in the house with one slave, Dean, to look after her. Her sons Drewry and John Jr. lived at neighboring farms. Kate hung around for a while, after John Bell's death, watching over Lucy, who she had always treated with kindness.

Before making her exit Kate told Lucy she would return in seven years. True to her word, Kate returned, mainly visiting John Bell Jr. Though never having much time for the entity, they spoke of world affairs with Kate making quite accurate predictions of the forthcoming American Civil War in 1861. After three weeks, the Bell Witch departed, saying she would visit the descendants of the Bell family in 107 years. That would have been in 1935, but there are no reports that Kate made direct contact. Five generations on, Bell descendants claim to have had some unusual experiences.

Lucy Bell died in the house in 1837 at 69-years-old. She is buried in the private old Bell Cemetery. The home was raised in the 1940's. Red River Station was renamed Adams in 1898 after a local businessman. Part of the town is more a museum of deserted houses, and a log cabin from the Bell farm was relocated there. Being small, it was probably housing for the slaves.

There are several caves in the area. One being on the Bell property is thought to be where Kate took refuge and still resides. Being of historical interest with its Indian cave drawings, it is open at certain times to the public and for paranormal investigations.

Of the nine children of John and Lucy Bell, Jesse was their first born in 1790. He married Martha Gunn in September 1817 and had 9 children. Jesse was in his fifties when he moved his family to Mississippi to become a successful farmer. He died in 1843.

John Jr. was the second child born in 1793. He married Elizabeth Gunn in 1928 and had 6 children. Building a house just south of his childhood home, John accumulated over 600 acres of land to become a farmer and magistrate. He died from pneumonia in 1862.

Drewry Bell, born in 1796, never married. He farmed land across the river from the Bell property. It's said the trauma of growing up suffering the poltergeist activity affected him all his life. He died on January 1, 1865.

Esther Bell was born in 1800, being the eldest daughter and the first of the Bell children to marry. She was also the first to see the apparition of the witch in human form. She married Alexander Porter in July 1817, being spared most of the activity in the Bell home. She had 12 children, most dying in childhood. The Porter's moved to

Mississippi in the late 1830s, and Esther died there in 1859.

The fifth child, Zadock, was born in 1803, being no more than a baby when the family moved to Red River. It's thought that he was away at boarding school to further his education to become a lawyer during the Bell Witch years. In 1821 he married Katherine Lawrence and moved to Alabama where there was a pandemic. He then moved to Florida to set up practice only for the pandemic to follow. He died from fever at the age of 23.

Betsy Bell, the 6th child, remained at what is now Cedar Hill after her husband's death, it only being 4-miles from her family home. When her health began to decline, around 1874, she moved to Mississippi to live with her daughter, Eliza. She wouldn't talk about what she had gone through, it continuing for a year after her father's death. She was always too scared to sleep on her own and would sleep with one of her grandchildren. Betsy died on July 11, 1888, aged 82.

Richard Bell, the 7th child, was born at the Bell farm in 1811. He was married three times and had two children, living his whole life in Red River as a successful farmer. Richard was only 6 years old when the family troubles began but years later wrote an account of his experiences. His son, Allen Bell showed the manuscript to several people that ended up being published as "An Authenticated History of the Bell Witch" by Martin Ingram in 1894. The manuscript as never been made public, leading many to believe it may not exist. Richard bought a house from his younger brother that sat beside the Red River, living there for two years before his death in 1890. He is buried in the Bell Cemetery.

Joel Bell was the youngest child born in 1813. Being no more than 4-year-old, he only learned about Kate from listening to family recollections. He used stones and timber from his childhood home to build a house half a mile away at Brown's Ford Bluff, which he sold to his brother Richard when he moved to Springfield, Tennessee. It's said that some strange occurrences happened at the house. He married twice, having 14 children when he died in 1890.

With superstition and outright lies long after the events, it's only the now long-dead witnesses that could make more sense of what happened at the Bell family home and the surrounding area of Red

River.

It's not difficult to surmise that someone could have used a mild haunting that's been embellished over the years to commit murder.

BLACK AGGIE

Black Aggie Statue
copyright J W Ocker.

The statue of a cloaked, hooded figure once overlooked a prominent grave at the Druid Ridge Cemetery, Pikesville, Maryland. Apart from gaining a gruesome reputation, it is a copy. The original was commissioned by Henry Adams, the grandson of President John Quincy Adams that can be found at Rock Creek Cemetery, Washington, DC. The bronze artwork took Augustus Saint-Gaudens four years to produce to the specification of Henry Adams. It was then given the title "The Mystery of the Hereafter and The Peace of God that Passeth Understanding," but quickly became more commonly known as "Grief," a name Adams detested.

Being erected in 1891, six years after the death of his wife, Marion Adams, nicknamed Clover, who committed suicide, it soon began to attract attention. Henry Adams joined her in 1918. It is said the statue is neither male nor female, and becoming a tourist attraction, was listed on the National Register of Historic Places in 1972.

No one knows who commissioned the illegal copy bought by Felix Agnus for his family plot. Henry Adams received many requests to produce copies, but always refused, including using photographs for commercial purposes. He was made aware of the Agnus statue in 1908, one year after it was erected at the Baltimore cemetery where Felix Agnus's mother, Anne, had been interred in 1880. This brought disputes between Adams and Agnus. Augustus Saint-Gaudens had died the year before, but his widow Augusta joined the campaign to have the statue removed. Unfortunately, there was a snag when going to court as Saint-Gaudens hadn't copyrighted his work. Agnus won the case and was awarded $4,500 but agreed to destroy his statue, obviously going back on his word. However, the sculptor, Edward Pausch, who had completed many notable works, lost his case against Augusta Saint-Gaudens along with his reputation.

Stories of the Agnus statue being cursed soon spread as it locally became known as "Black Aggie." Presumed female, it was said that her eyes glowed red at night, and anyone seeing them would go blind. Grass didn't grow on the plot, and if a pregnant woman walked in the shadow of the statue, it was said she would lose the baby. Then there was its attraction to other spirits, from those buried at Druids Ridge Cemetery to Clover Adams.

Teenagers used the statue as an initiation rite that anyone sitting on her lap and remaining overnight meant inevitable death. A popular urban legend associated with Black Aggie entwines the Bloody Mary myth. Instead, anyone looking in a mirror and saying Black Aggie three times would summon up the image of the statue.

A story with several variations is of a boy who for his pledge, was dared to sit on Black Aggie's lap. Two boys accompanied him to make sure the deed was carried out. As the boy climbed onto her knee, the two boys saw the eyes of the statue turning to a red glow as her arms encircled him. They ran screaming from the scene, making so much noise that the cemetery caretaker went to investigate. The statue looked the same as usual, but resting on its lap was a boy, his face a mask of the terror he experienced in death.

The many urban legends soon began to attract nighttime visitors. With vandalism and late-night break-ins, depending on which story is believed, from the cemetery, having had enough of the trespassers, to the Agnus family being concerned over the graffiti, in 1967 Black Aggie was donated to the Smithsonian Museum. The grave is now left with only the plinth bearing the Agnus name and an inscription for General Felix Agnus.

Realizing the statue was an unofficial copy, the Smithsonian didn't put Black Aggie on public display, leading many to ask its whereabouts only to receive vague answers. This allowed conspiracy theories to grow that it had been destroyed. But then, in 1997, Black

Aggie was discovered by a college student who was also a reporter for his school's newspaper. Black Aggie had been sitting peacefully in the courtyard at the rear of the Dolly Madison House at Lafayette Square since 1987. Ironically Black Aggie has ended up close to where Clover Adams died and is said to haunt.

BLUFF CREEK BIGFOOT

Bluff Creek 6 Streams National Park, California. Artwork Diane Browne copyright 2022.

Stories of a large, hairy creature go back further than when white men and women colonized and invaded the tribal lands of America. Like pop and soda, it usually depends on the area as to whether it's Bigfoot or Sasquatch. There is even the theory that they are a race of alien visitors leaving behind no artefacts to excuse the lack of proof.

In 1958, Andrew Genzoli, a journalist for the Humboldt Times at Eureka, California, received a letter from a reader reporting mysterious large footprints found in northern California. Printing the name "Bigfoot" as a fun story, national newspapers and TV news stations picked up on the article for the legend to spread. Like searching for ghosts, there have been many Bigfoot hoaxes, producing faked evidence to find notoriety and make a little money along the way. With the aid of social media, channels are uploading dubious evidence at best while garnering donations and selling merchandise.

Sightings are reported all over the United States and well over the border into Canada. Most reports come from the western states of California and Washington. Searching for a glimpse of the creature is a hobby for some, while for others it's an obsession. Groups have been foundered in an attempt to find evidence, producing casts of footprints along with photographs and film footage. In 1976, a Bigfoot researcher sent fifteen hairs attached to a piece of skin to the FBI. The FBI don't usually do testing beyond criminal cases but will make the exception to help in scientific and research fields. Not realizing the effect their good deed would have, on declassifying the file after 40 years, conspiracy theories quickly sprang up that the government was studying Bigfoot. Unfortunately, the sample they received turned out to be from a deer.

In 2008, a car salesman and a police officer in Georgia hit the news headlines when they claimed to have found the body of a Bigfoot. Rick Dyer and officer Matt Whitton made a guest spot on a radio show to tell their story of finding the body of a Bigfoot while out hiking which they had put on ice, producing proof in the form of grainy film footage. The hoax became bigger than the two men could have imagined. However, they continued with the story until it became obvious that it was no more than a costume the men had filled with roadkill and meat from a slaughterhouse.

Matt Whitton lost his job with the Clayton County Police Department while Rick Dyer went on to perpetrate another Bigfoot hoax in 2012, claiming to have shot and killed one of the creatures in San Antonio, Texas, choosing a state where it's not illegal to kill a Bigfoot.

The most famous Bigfoot sighting came in 1967 when Roger Patterson filmed a biped creature at Bluff Creek in northern California. Over the years, the film has been studied as new technology comes along.

After reading an article in 1961, Roger Patterson became fascinated with Bigfoot. Whenever he heard of a sighting, he travelled to the area to find anyone willing to talk about Bigfoot, mainly lumberjacks who showed him large footprints. Patterson spent hours searching for any evidence and in 1966 self-published a paperback, "Do Abominable Snowmen of America Really Exist?" in the hope of selling enough copies to fund an expedition. Learning that a construction crew had their machinery damaged and large footprints had been found around the worksite, Patterson talked his skeptical friend, Bob Gimlin into accompanying him on a trek. Gimlin wasn't interested in Bigfoot hunting but was intrigued enough to want to see the footprints. The two men entered the Six Rivers National Forest that covers a million acres of wilderness.

Roger Patterson had a cine camera to film evidence of Bigfoot and film some of the scenery. It was around 1pm on October 20, 1967, when they reached the creek. The horses became skittish with Patterson's mount rearing.

Dismounting, Patterson grabbed the camera from his saddlebag as he had spotted movement. Shouting to Gimlin to cover him, he cocked his rifle as Patterson began to film a creature walking along the creek to look directly at the camera as it went towards a clump of trees and out of sight. Patterson estimated that the closest he got was around 25 feet. The film lasts just under one minute and has become the equivalent of the Zapruder film of the John F. Kennedy assassination.

The story of the two men caused a wide divide between those who believe and those who are just as obsessed with debunking the myth. Many books and articles have been written, including claims that Bigfoot was no more than a man in a suit named Bob Hieronimus who claimed he wore a suit for the filming. Philip Morris, a costume maker, also claimed he made the suit for Roger Patterson but couldn't provide any receipts. When asked to reproduce the costume, it looked nothing like depicted in what is often called the Patterson-Gimlin, and even the Patty film.

Many people later visited Bluff Creek and continue to do so, claiming to have taken pictures and made plaster casts of large footprints.

Roger Patterson continued to hunt for Bigfoot and teamed up with his brother-in-law, Al DeAtley, taking the film on tour to acquire funds to set up an expedition to return to Bluff Creek. Though people claim to have discredited the film, at the time of this printing the film has not been debunked. However, Roger Patterson was making what he called a documentary before the Bluff Creek incident, leading to allegations that it was a movie with the storyline of five cowboys hunting down a Bigfoot, and so a costume to represent Bigfoot would be needed. It may or may not have gotten that far as funding ran out, and the movie was never made.

Roger Patterson was 38 years old when he died from cancer in 1971. He founded the Northwest Research Foundation with donations and the lecture circuit funding several expeditions. On Patterson's death, Ron Olson took over the organization and changed the name to the North American Wildlife Research Association.

Bob Gimlin was cut out of further deals and didn't have any further communication with Roger Patterson until the latter part of his life. The splintered groups on one side wanting to hear his story to the other calling him an outright liar took its toll. He always claimed it was true but avoided any publicity. He found himself the center of attention after the death of Roger Patterson, which almost cost him his marriage. However, after 35 years of ridicule from non-believers, in 2003, Bob Gimlin spoke at a conference and continues to give interviews. Gimlin also took a role in David D Ford's 2021 movie, "Man vs Bigfoot."

With no positive proof that Bigfoot exists any more than proving it doesn't, only four states have laws making it illegal to kill a Bigfoot, being Washington, West Virginia, Wyoming, and Wisconsin. Whether you believe in Bigfoot or not, the debate will continue for decades to come.

THE COTTINGLEY FAIRIES

Elsie Wright with a winged gnome 1918. Photograph by Frances Griffiths.

Cottingley is a village in West Yorkshire, England, where, in 1917 two girls claimed they played with fairies at the bottom of the garden. Elsie Wright was 16-years-old and her cousin Frances Griffiths 9-years of age when they borrowed a camera from Elsie's father and took two pictures of the small sprites.

Arthur Wright developed the plates himself, and seeing the fairies, thought them no more than a prank using cardboard cutouts. Borrowing the camera for a second time, the girls took one plate that showed Elsie with a small human-shaped creature standing upon her hand.

Edward Gardner, member of the Theosophical Society of London.

After this, Arthur Wright refused to lend them the camera again, but his wife, Polly, was convinced the girls were really playing with fairies by the stream which ran along the bottom of their garden.

It was a year later that Frances wrote to a friend in South Africa enclosing a photo of her with the fairies, writing on the back that she never saw them in South Africa but maybe it was too hot for them.

Polly Wright didn't keep her belief in the fairies to herself. Learning that there was a lecture at the Theological Society on Fairy Life was an opportunity she couldn't let pass by. At the end of the lecture, she approached the speaker, Edward Gardner and showed him two of the pictures, agreeing that they could be used at the society's annual conference. Many people claim to have seen fairies but two girls being able to catch them on camera drew attention.

The photographs and glass plate negatives were expertly examined by Harold Snelling and declared to be genuine in that the negatives had not been tampered with. However, he did not go so far as to say the pictures contained fairies, but that the camera had reproduced what was in front of the lens. He also made copies of the negatives which he printed for Gardner who sold them at his lectures.

In 1920, Sherlock Holmes author, Arthur Conan Doyle came into the picture. It was by chance that he learned of the fairies at Cottingley when he was commissioned to write a story for a Christmas edition of The Strand Magazine. Doyle wrote to the Wright family to ask permission to use a picture to go with his short story. Arthur Wright, still being skeptical agreed but refused to take any money.

Arthur Conan Doyle. Photographer Arnold Genthe.

The article appeared in December 1920, and within days, the magazine sold out. To protect the identity of the girls, their names were changed with Elsie given the name Iris and Frances, Alice. In the meantime, Edward Gardner and Arthur Conan Doyle had the plates examined by Kodak, where several technicians examined them and came back with the same results as Snelling. The plates had not been tampered with but had only given an image of what the camera saw. They could not give the men what they wanted, which was to certify the reality of the fairies. A third company was sought which reported that the plates had been tampered with in some way, making the photos fake.

Gardner arranged, with the agreement of the Wright family, for the girls to take more photographs. By this time, Frances was living in Scarborough but went to stay with the Wright's during the summer holidays. Gardner supplied two cameras and plates and the girls were

Frances Griffiths with fairies 1917.
Photographer Elsie Wright.

left alone while Mrs. Wright went to visit her sister. And so, the girls went to the stream, producing several more pictures.

These appeared years later in a book by Edward Gardner titled "Fairies: A Book of Real Fairies". By this time, there had been many critics who apart from pointing out that fairies were no more than fairytales, it was thought the hairstyles were very modern.

Interest in the Cottingley fairies soon faded. Elsie and Frances grew into young women and married. Then in 1966, a reporter sought out Elsie, who said she believed she had photographed her thoughts. The article appeared in the Daily Express newspaper, bringing refreshed interest from a new generation. In 1976 Elsie and Frances appeared on Yorkshire television, now much older at the ages of 75 and 69 respectively. They agreed that it was reasonable to deny the existence of fairies but continued to insist that the photographs were real.

In 1978, the American debunker James Randi became involved in the continuing debate, examining the photographs with modern methods of the computer. Enhancing the images, it was declared that threads could be seen holding up the fairies. However, it was George Crowley, a photographer and editor of the Bristol Journal of Photography who interviewed Elsie in 1983. She admitted it was a hoax and Crowley published that the photos were fake. Shortly after, Elsie and Frances finally came clean in an interview published in The Unexplained magazine. Elsie was always very talented when it came to artwork, which is why her father thought she had made the fairies. Elsie had copied illustrations from children's books onto cardboard, adding wings to make them look like the more traditional belief of what fairies looked like. Cutting them out, they then held them upright with hat pins, not thread. Though admitting the photos were fake, they both continued to say they did see fairies by the stream.

There was also a dispute between the cousins where Frances said she took a photo becoming known as "Fairies at the Sun Bath." She distinctly remembered that it was a rainy day, and Elsie hadn't set anything up. Frances said she took the photograph only for the plate to reveal what looked like fairies, but Elsie said they were all fake. They would no doubt have revealed their prank much earlier except for Arthur Conan Doyle. They knew how much he wanted to believe the photographs were real and was ridiculed for it. By the time Elsie made a written statement that it had been no more than a hoax, the nine pages now being on display at the National Science and Media Museum in Bradford, Doyle had been dead over 50 years.

Despite the admission by both ladies that the photographs had been nothing more than fun, many still believe the Cottingley fairies to be real. Unfortunately, this led people to the stream on fairy hunts, leaving rubbish and destroying the original beauty of the place.

Frances died in 1986, and Elsie followed two years later in 1988, leaving behind a story of fairies some still believe to be true.

CRYBABY BRIDGES

Governors Bridge, Davidsonville, Nr Bowie, Maryland

There are many crybaby bridges around America, all with similar themes. Now permanently closed, Governor's Bridge on Governor Bridge Road in Maryland is better known by locals as the Crybaby Bridge. Crossing the Patuxent River, the single-lane truss bridge is in Davidsonville, Prince George's County. The story isn't an old urban legend like most, dating back to the 1950s. It was on a foggy night that a woman crossing the bridge was struck by a car. The driver was none other than her husband, who hadn't been able to see her until it was too late. Typical of crybaby bridges, she was carrying their baby that fell into the river below and can now be heard crying. Another version involves the Ku Klux Klan using the bridge to kill and dispose of black children. Whatever the reason, people who cross the bridge claim to have heard the crying of a child coming from the river below.

The Crybaby Bridge at Anderson in South Carolina now runs alongside a newly built bridge being part of High Shoals Road. It's said the bridge was haunted before it was completed when one of the construction workers fell to his death. After the accident, workers said the bridge would creak and groan like a man crying. To allay their fears, the excuse given was the spans settling. In 1919 it was taken to Charleston, where it remained in use until 1952, having gained a reputation with it being said that dogs wouldn't cross it and birds wouldn't perch upon it. It also creaked and groaned when vehicles used it. Three years after the bridge arrived at Anderson, it became known as Crybaby Bridge. Though the bridge is now closed, the legend persists that an unmarried mother threw her baby into the water below. She was found weeks later hanging in a barn. It was one year after the tragic event that nearby residents reported hearing the sound of a baby's cries coming from the area of the bridge. Apart from the sound of a baby crying, a woman was often seen on the bridge before it was abandoned. Sightings of the lady in white often resulted in engines stalling to headlights going out.

What is thought to be the original Crybaby Bridge on Whitesville Road, just south of Columbus in Harris County, Georgia, has been demolished and replaced. However, the legend remains with three stories of children being killed but the most common is of a poor farmer with a large family. When his wife found herself pregnant for the fifth time, the farmer couldn't afford another mouth to feed and, without telling his wife, paid the doctor to get rid of it. As soon as the baby was born, the doctor took it and threw it from the bridge. A ghostly woman is also said to haunt the area, being the baby's mother. There have been many over the years who on a dark night have parked on the bridge and followed the instructions to sprinkle baby powder around the vehicle. With the engine and lights off, after 10 minutes, look at the powder where there will be baby footprints. It's a popular spot for teenagers, especially around Halloween, and so a time of year to avoid the place.

Sleepy Hollow Road at Prospect, Kentucky, has a bridge where children can be heard crying. They are said to be the victims of a satanic cult that sacrificed children as part of their bloody rites in throwing them from the bridge into Harrod's Creek. Most of the road is said to have paranormal activity. Being a wooded country lane with no streetlights can make for an eerie night-time drive, and with the ghost stories thrown on top, a scary experience to heighten the senses. Other legends include a black car that tries to run vehicles off the road and there is alleged to be a time warp with anyone travelling along the road suddenly finding that watches have jumped forward in time, losing up to two hours.

There are a few crybaby bridges in Ohio, the state being abound in urban legends and hauntings. At Rogue's Hollow on Hametown Road, a crying child can be heard along with the reenactment of a woman dropping her baby over the bridge into Silver Creek. Another more modern story is of a car that skidded on ice and plunged into the water. The people were killed, and when their bodies were removed a baby was unknowingly left in the car where it starved to death.

The ghost of a woman in white is said to haunt Helltown Crybaby Bridge at Peninsula on Boston Mills Road, being a young mother who got rid of her baby on the bridge over the Cuyahoga River, which is next to the Boston Mill Visitor Centre. There doesn't appear to be any reports of a crying baby, but the ritual was to drive to the middle of the bridge and park, leaving the keys in the car. Moving away from the vehicle and taking a walk, making sure to have a spare key because on returning, the engine would be running, and the doors locked. It isn't advised to do this now as there are no parking signs all over the town, including the bridge. This suburb of Boston, Ohio, at one time, was teeming with urban legends that sprang up in the 1970s after the government decided to oust the people as part of a national park project. With little compensation using loopholes to say they didn't own the land; it was then left to become a ghost town. Conspiracy theorists concluded that the people were really moved because of a toxic chemical spill that created mutants, including a huge man-eating python. There were stories of satanic rites, human sacrifices, and hauntings in each abandoned house. Becoming a dumping ground, including toxic waste, the area was

Schrader Road Tunnel Brdge, Ohio beneath railroad tracks beside Lick Run. Photo credit Ohio Exploration Society.

cleaned up and the houses torn down in 2016.

Ohio even has its own Crybaby Tunnel. This is a double underpass bridge with a rail track running above and two tunnels, one for the road and the other for Paint Creek. There are two versions of the legend, but the best known is that of a woman who on a hot summer evening was driven to despair when her baby wouldn't stop crying. Instead of trying to discover what was wrong, she placed her baby on the railway track where it cried for hours before a train came and ended its misery. Now on summer nights, those driving along Schrader Road in Chillicothe and slowing down through the tunnel can hear the cries of the baby overhead. For a more dangerous thrill (not advised), it's said the headlights should be turned off and the windows wound down.

Another state with many haunted bridges is Oklahoma. The steel bridge going over Lake Overholser on Overholser Drive beside route 66 is said to be a crybaby bridge which is the haunt of a White Lady holding a baby. People have claimed to have approached her thinking she requires help, only for her to disappear. However, it's more common to hear the cries of a baby. The legend goes that if a car parks on the bridge and turns the lights out, or even braver, for someone to walk over the bridge at night, they may see the White Lady.

The Van Sant Crybaby Bridge over Pidcock Creek on Covered Bridge Road at New Hope, Pennsylvania, comes with a sad story. The legend is of a young girl who hung herself on the bridge after throwing her baby into the creek when she was disowned by her family and spurned by her lover. Apart from that, the covered bridge is also reputed to have been used in the lynching of horse thieves.

THE CURSED CAR

Archduke Franz Ferdinand &
Sophie, Duchess of Hohenberg.

It is said that WW1 was sparked by the assassination of the heir to the Austria-Hungary throne.

Archduke Franz Ferdinand Carl Ludwig Joseph Maria of Austria was one of the wealthiest men in the country, besides being Emperor in waiting. Maybe his trip to England in November 1913 was a premonition of what was to come. The Archduke and his wife Sophie spent a week at Windsor Castle with King George V and Queen Mary before spending a further week at Welbeck Abbey in Nottinghamshire with the Duke of Portland. As the Archduke was a big and small game hunter, his host arranged a hunt on the Welbeck estate. At some point, one of the laborer's carrying a loaded gun stumbled and fell, discharging both barrels, the first missing the Archduke by a whisker.

The following year on June 28, 1914, Franz and Sophie went to Sarajevo, a part of the Austria-Hungary empire, to inspect troops of the imperial armed forces. The annexation to Austria in 1908 didn't sit well with Serbians who felt that Sarajevo should be part of Serbia. The governor was warned that security was insufficient but refused to bring out the army, leaving 60 police officers to secure the city and control the crowds turning out to welcome the Archduke. No one was aware that six assassins armed with bombs were lying in wait along the route from the train station. The first assassin failed to act. The second also let the procession go by, but the third carried out his orders. The bomb bounced off the back of the royal car, exploding beneath the following vehicle, wounding around twenty people.

After resting at Governor Oskar Potiorek's residence, the couple insisted on visiting the hospital to check on the wounded.

Having learned that the assassination had failed, 19-year-old Gavrilo Princip planned to ambush the car when the Archduke left. However, he wouldn't have to wait that long. It had been decided to change the route to avoid the crowds, but the driver hadn't been told and taking a wrong turn, the governor ordered him to stop. The driver reversed but stalled the engine directly across the road from a cafe where Princip was sitting.

Quickly taking advantage of his good fortune, Princip walked up to the car and pulled out a pistol. Before anyone could stop him, he shot Sophie in the stomach and then Franz in the neck.

The last words of Franz Ferdinand were, "Don't die, darling, live for our children." Thinking the assassination had failed yet again, the car returned to the governor's house for medical treatment, but both died enroute.

Twenty-five men accused of being involved in the assassination plot were rounded up. Being put on trial, they were charged with high treason, coming with the sentence of death. Some of the defendants claimed they were unwilling participants, that possibly being why the first two assassins refrained from using their bombs. All claimed they were terrorists, but the court didn't believe they worked as a lone group and were found guilty of espionage in collusion with Serbia. Nine were acquitted, five received the death sentence and hanged, while the rest received prison sentences from three years to life. Princip was sentenced to 20 years but died on April 28, 1918, from tuberculosis, put down to the poor conditions at the Terezin fort prison.

The trial led to accusations that Serbia was to blame for the assassination and the countries prepared for war. Russia was an ally of Serbia with France and Great Britain. Austria-Hungary had the support of Germany and Italy. If other countries had kept out, it would have saved millions of lives and possibly been a short war.

Now we come to the cursed car in which Franz and Sophie died. The Gräf & Stift Double Phaeton was loaned by Count Von Heirek for the royal visit. Stories arose, most of which cannot be confirmed other than its end. The stories seem to have become popular in the 1950s, being added to with time.

The first person to come into possession of the car after the assassination; was none other than Oskar Potiorak, the former governor. He went on to fight in the war, believing he was saved from the assassination to avenge the deaths. The urban legend is that he died in an insane asylum. The truth is, he survived the war, retired, and died in 1933 at the age of 80, never owning the car.

The second owner was a captain in the army who died in an accident, killing two pedestrians in the process. It was then owned by the Governor of Yugoslavia, ironically Serbia being a part of the kingdom. With its internal struggles, there may not have been a governorship post. However, the governor is said to have had four accidents, losing an arm in the last. The car was fully restored and came into possession of Doctor Srikis, who didn't believe in curses, but after six months the car was found overturned with the doctors stricken body beneath it. The car was restored once more, and another doctor took possession but soon found that his patients didn't want a doctor visiting them in a cursed car. With his practice dwindling, he sold it to a Swiss racing driver who entered a road race in the Dolomites where another accident killed the driver, breaking his neck. It then passed into the hands of a farmer when one day it stalled. With the help of another farmer towing it, the engine is said to have come to life, ramming the car towing it and killing both men. With another restoration, the next owner, Tiber Hirschfield, changed the blood-red color to blue, but this didn't stop the curse. Inviting friends to a wedding party, the new owner set off with his guests only for all the occupants to die in a head-on collision. Rebuilt once more, the car was placed in a museum where the attendant told stories of the deaths and the curse to curious visitors but wouldn't allow anyone to sit behind the wheel. During WW2, the museum was struck in a bombing raid. When the rubble was cleared, there was no sign of the museum attendant or the car.

The true story is that after the assassination, the car was taken to the Heeresgeschichtilches Museum in Vienna, where it is to this day, being a main attraction in its original green color.

Graf and Stift Double Phaeton assassination car on display at the Heeresgeschchtliches Museum.

THE CURSED FILM SCRIPT

The Incomparable Atuk book cover.

"The Incomparable Atuk" was published in 1963, being retitled "Stick Your Neck Out" for American readers. The novel is a comedy penned by Canadian author Mordecai Richler who died July 3, 2001, at 70 years old.

In the 1980s, the copyright was acquired, turned into a screenplay and shortened to "Atuk," being Inuit for grandfather. The story follows the life of a pot-bellied Canadian Eskimo more interested in writing poetry than working and hunting to support the village. When an opportunity comes along to see his daydreams come true, Atuk runs away to the city of Toronto, which may as well be a different planet.

The adapted story for the film changed the location to New York. The script was ready to go into production once a somewhat overweight comedy actor was found to play Atuk.

One of the first actors to like the script was John Belushi, who was committed to playing the character.

Unfortunately, John died on March 5, 1982, at the young age of 33. After years of struggling with a drug addiction, with the help of family and friends, he was winning the battle.

After being clean of drugs for months, he relapsed when a drug dealer, Cathy Smith, not only sold him what is called a speedball, a combination of heroin and cocaine but administered it to him by needle no more than 11 times. As he lay dead or dying, Smith fled the scene and was later arrested for a non-related incident. She eventually pled guilty to manslaughter and, after serving 15 months in prison, was deported to her homeland of Canada, where she died aged-73 on August 16, 2020.

The next to pick up the script was Pentecostal preacher turned standup comedian and actor Sam Kinison who, like John Belushi, had spots on "Saturday Night Live."

This time the production got underway with Sam filming a few scenes, but he quickly became disillusioned when he was wrongly told he had control over the script. Being unable to make the changes he wanted, he walked away with legal proceedings pending in the contract dispute. The film was put on hold while Sam fulfilled other commitments. He had been married and divorced twice and looking at third time lucky, on April 4, 1992, married Moroccan actress and make-up artist, Malika Souiri.

Six days later, on the 10th, he and his new wife were on their way to perform at the Riverside Resort Hotel and Casino in Laughlin, Nevada. Sam was driving along Needles Highway being around 30 miles from the casino when his vehicle was hit head-on by a pickup truck driven by a 17-year-old drunk driver.

Sam Kinison wasn't wearing a seatbelt which could have saved his life. When emergency services arrived, he was still alive. His last words were, "I don't want to die. I don't want to die." The 38-year-old comedian was pronounced dead at the scene.

Malika was severely injured and rushed to hospital. She eventually recovered, going on to act in several films. She married actor Paul Borghese in September 1995, and remains happily married.

The next comedy actor to take an interest in the part of Atuk was

John Candy. He was negotiating several projects, looking to get the role of Ignatius J. Reilly, the lead character in the comedy novel "A Confederacy of Dunces" by John Kennedy Toole. He was also looking to portray Roscoe "Fatty" Arbuckle in a planned biographical film covering the life of the silent movie star who had his career cut short when he was accused of raping starlet Virginia Rappe, leading to her death. Along with Atuk, those two scripts have also been put on the shelf to gather dust.

John Candy. Artwork copyright Diane Browne 2022

John Candy was only 43 years old when he died in Mexico on March 4, 1994. Apart from being overweight, mainly caused by binge eating, cocaine use and being a heavy smoker and drinker contributed to his heart attack, along with genetic heart problems.

He had already narrated some of the script of a character, a turkey called Redfeather for the Disney cartoon "Pocahontas." On John Candy's death, Redfeather was removed from the film and replaced with Meeka, a raccoon voiced by John Kassir.

Being the third actor to show interest in Atuk will forever link John Candy to the curse.

Other actors looked at the script with some turning it down as a curse became linked to the screenplay.

Will Ferrell would have been a younger and thinner Atuk. Jack Black is said to have turned it down though John Goodman and Josh Mostel showed an interest along with Jonathan Winters being the oldest actor approached.

In 1997, Chris Farley was in negotiations to play Atuk. Having read the script, he was ready to accept when he died from a drug overdose. His death on December 18, 1997, was compared to John Belushi with an autopsy finding that it was a speedball of cocaine and morphine that ended his life at the age of 33.

Chris was also in talks to join the cast alongside John Candy for "A

Confederacy of Dunces," leading those with a persuasion towards superstitions to believe the film script was cursed. He had also recorded over 80% of the narration as the famous green ogre, Shrek. The producers felt it in better taste to recast, and fellow Saturday Night Live comedy actor, Mike Myers made the character his own.

Phil Hartman was rumored to be interested. On May 27, 1998, in a drug and alcohol haze, his wife Brynn Hartman shot Phil three times as he slept in their bed. The first shot between the eyes would have instantly killed him. After confessing what she had done, she locked herself in the bedroom and killed herself with either the same gun or a different revolver, leaving two orphaned children.

Robin Williams was approached but evidently couldn't find the time or wasn't interested. His name has been associated with the Atuk curse but production had long been shelved when he took his own life on August 11, 2014. That is if he did, but that's another story.

DR. CRIPPEN - AN INNOCENT MAN!

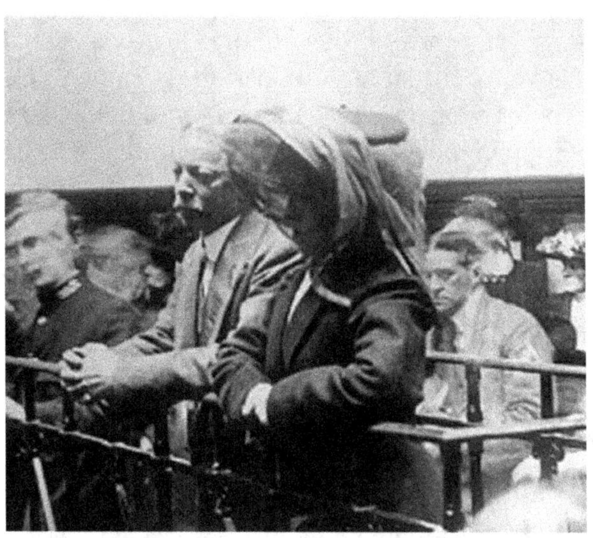

Dr. Crippen and Ethel Le Neve at Bow Street court prior to separate trials. Bain News Service.

It became one of the most notorious trials of the 20th century when Doctor Hawley Harvey Crippen (48) and Ethel Clara Neave, known as Ethel Le Neve (27), were charged with the murder of Crippen's wife. And Dr Crippen continues to be as celebrated a killer as Jack the Ripper, who committed his crimes twelve years earlier in London in 1888.

Crippen was an American citizen born in Michigan on September 11, 1862, being the only surviving child of Myron and Ardesee Crippen.

He attended the University of Michigan Homeopathic Medical School and Cleveland Homeopathic Medical College, earning his doctorate in 1884. He married an Irish nurse, Charlotte Jane Bell, and the couple had a son, Hawley Otto Crippen, who was 4-years-old when his mother suffered a stroke while pregnant. Both she and the child died.

29-year-old Crippen, now a widower, sent his son to live with his parents in California. He then moved to New York, setting up his own practice and remarried around two years later. This new lady in his life was totally different, being obsessed with achieving a career on the stage. Kunigunde Mackamotzki had changed her name to Cora Turner, though her stage name was Belle Elmore. She was also 19-years-old, which may have been an ego boost for Crippen. For Cora, the attraction of being married to a doctor would have brought some prestige and Crippen, being a mild-mannered man, was easy for her to control. Cora continued to pursue her career with singing and acting lessons, failing to make any headway in becoming an opera singer. Then came the American depression of 1893, leading to the closure of theaters and leaving Crippen with fewer patients. When Crippen closed his surgery, Cora was forced to live below the standards to which she had become accustomed.

Dr. Harvey Hawley Crippen.

He soon found a job as a consultant for a mail-order company selling homoeopathic remedies. By 1895 he was the area manager in Philadelphia and two-years later was sent to London to open an overseas office. Cora remained in Philadelphia to continue her acting lessons and doing the social rounds. She arrived in London four months later to try her hand on the English stage.

Unfortunately, Cora doesn't appear to have had much talent. Her husband gave way to her demands to the point of it affecting his work. He was not only financially supporting Cora's efforts to become a star, but also became her manager. When his name appeared in a Theater program, Dr Munyon's pharmaceutical company, who had sent Crippen to England, let him go. This meant the Crippen's had to tighten the purse strings. In September 1905, they moved from Piccadilly to Islington, leasing 39 Hilldrop Crescent in Holloway, no longer standing after being bombed during World War 2. They took in lodgers to prop-up Cora's lifestyle of clothes, jewelry and hair dye, which her husband often did for her, turning the dark roots a bright auburn.

Cora soon made friends among the thespian set and became treasurer of the Music Hall Ladies Guild. Their meetings were held in the same building where Crippen had found a job making up remedies ordered by mail. Although he was a doctor, his license wouldn't allow him to practice or write out prescriptions in Britain.

Kunigunde Mackamotzki aka Cora Turner, Belle Elmore and Mrs Crippen.

The marriage wasn't going well, and by the time they moved to Hilldrop Crescent, they had separate bedrooms. It's alleged that Cora had relationships with some of the lodgers, besides a married theater actor and real estate agent, Brian Miller. It's said that Miller gave Cora money, allowing her to delay following her husband to England.

On January 31, 1910, theatrical friends, Clara and Paul Martinetti, were invited for dinner. Mr. Martinetti was feeling ill and at 1.30am decided to leave, even though Cora offered them a bed for the night. That was the last time anyone, apart from her husband, saw Cora Crippen.

From there, things became quite strange. Crippen visited the Martinetti's the next day to check on Paul's health. He told them and other friends that Cora had returned to America to care for a sick relative. Some thought it was to nurse Crippen's mother, though Ardesee Crippen had died a year before. Cora's friends became concerned because they hadn't heard from her. Crippen then went on to say Cora was ill and then that she had died.

Not only did he tell friends of Cora's demise and that she had been cremated but wrote a letter to her family with the news. To make matters worse, he had been in a relationship with his secretary, which started as a friendship around 1904. Crippen would take Ethel Le Neve out for dinner after work to delay going home. From there, the relationship blossomed.

Unfortunately, divorce wasn't so easy. Apart from being looked upon as scandalous, infidelity by the wife or husband had to be proved beyond doubt. Although Cora had alleged affairs with some of her lodgers, openly flirted with men in front of her husband, and was living with a man when she met Crippen, a divorce would brand her a woman of ill repute. On the other hand, if Crippen had declared having an affair with his secretary, it would have meant the end of his career.

Cora's friends became even more suspicious when Crippen moved his secretary into 39 Drophill Crescent. Ethel was also wearing Cora's furs and some of her jewelry. Six months after Cora's disappearance, Cora's friends went to the police with their suspicions that something had happened to her.

Chief Inspector Walter Dew visited Drophill Crescent, where he found Ethel, who told him she was the housekeeper. Crippen was at work, and Dew talked her into going with him so she couldn't telephone ahead and warn the doctor of his visit. All three returned to the house, and Dew was shown around with Crippen admitting that Cora had left him for an American actor. To cover the scandal and Cora's reputation, he had made up the story of her going to look after a sick relative and to her then dying.

Ethel Le Neve.

Dew had no reason not to believe Crippen. When the doctor told him he would place several newspaper adverts asking Cora to get in touch, Dew was satisfied. However, Inspector Dew had shaken Crippen, telling him that if Cora wasn't found, he would be in serious trouble. The next day, July 9, Crippen, who had already given notice to his landlord giving up the lease, sent out for a set of boy's clothes and with Ethel, fled the country. Under the names Mr. and Master Robinson, Crippen shaved off his moustache and began to grow a beard while wearing his glasses as little as possible. Ethel cut off her beautiful hair and dressed as a boy, passing herself off as her lover's son.

In the meantime, with pressure from Cora's friends, Inspector Dew returned to the house to find Crippen and Le Neve had gone. Dew relayed a description of the couple and took another look around no.39. The most obvious place to bury a body would be in the garden, and a search was duly undertaken. Then Dew turned his attention to the cellar. On his initial visit, he had poked around the edges of the cellar but this time, poked in the middle where there was some coal and stacked furniture. The poker he used easily went in between the bricks of the floor, producing a smell he was familiar with. Removing the bricks, they didn't uncover a whole body but human skin, a comb and some hair curlers.

It was unfortunate that Crippen chose to make his way to Canada by the Montrose, as Captain Henry George Kendall was taking an interest in the case. He became convinced that Mr. Robinson and his son were the pair the police were looking for. Much is still made of the fact that his telegraph messages led to the arrest, being the first of its kind. Captain Kendall received the reward money offered for the capture and arrest of Hawley Crippen and Ethel Le Neve, and Scotland Yard received a bill for the telegraph messages.

What doesn't make much sense is the so-called body in the cellar. The obvious conclusion was that it could be no one other than Cora. This was where she lived, and she was the only person reported missing. But it wasn't a corpse interred in the cellar but the remains of flesh, being described as filleted from the torso. There were no organs, no arms, legs or head, that have never been found.

The couple appeared in the dock together at Bow Street Court, where it was decided they should have separate trials. Dr Hawley Crippen was charged with murdering his wife and Ethel with accessory to murder.

The trial began at the Old Bailey on October 18, 1910, with no one in any doubt that Dr Crippen had murdered his wife and would be found guilty for it. Both sides called medical experts to give evidence that the layman would find hard to understand. Tests were carried out on what little evidence was collected, and it was put to the jury that Cora had been poisoned with hyoscine, a drug that is still commonly used today for travel sickness. It was estimated that there would have been enough to kill her. Not wishing to use up all the material on testing, the main tests to identify without any doubt that it was hyoscine were not carried out. Instead, it was tested on a cat, and the slides placed under a microscope looked like hyoscine. And anyway, it had to be hyoscine as with many other poisons used in homoeopathic remedies, Dr Crippen had bought a large quantity of hyoscine. Crippen even signed the poison book when making the purchase.

A small piece of skin containing a mark shaped like a boomerang, though the medical experts dubbed it a horseshoe, was brought into evidence. Witnesses for the prosecution claimed it was a scar from an operation Cora was known to have undertaken in America to have her ovaries removed, which would be the reason for her putting on weight once she arrived in London. It was suggested that instead of the usual method of folding out the skin to sew the incision, it was folded inwards. This wasn't proven as the surgeon who performed the operation wasn't located to give evidence. More qualified experts disagreed, claiming the skin was creased and had dried out in that position, making it look like a scar which was said to have some material trapped between the fold.

Though none of the experts could say whether the skin came from a male or female, the most damning evidence was a man's pajama top that the flesh was wrapped in. A representative of the manufacturer, "Jones Brothers Limited" told the court that by the label, it had been made in 1908 or later when they became a limited company. This threw out Crippen's claim that the body must already have been buried in the cellar when he and Cora moved there in September 1905.

It wasn't as such proven that poison was used to kill. Poison is more the choice of women with it being less gory, and with poison, the murderer doesn't even have to be present for their victim's demise. A statement was made that Ethel Le Neve had spent hours at a library studying poisons, but this wasn't presented at her trial.

There is no doubt that Crippen would have known of much better poisons that would make his wife ill until she faded away. Barring that, an accident, falling down the stairs, or even suicide would have been just as effective. Yet Dr Crippen, who had spent his career treating people in his own practice, at hospitals and gaining knowledge on mental health from working at an asylum, was accused of poisoning his wife and chopping her up in bits. Hawley Crippen's training involved ears, eyes, nose and throat, in which he specialized. He was a doctor, not a surgeon and never carried out any operations. There was no indication that he was a hunter where he could learn to cut up animal carcasses. Cutting up a body is time-consuming and no tools were produced that could have been used to perform the task. The prosecution didn't have the whole body and used the skin found in the cellar to present their evidence. Crippen's lawyers did little to help their client and the newspapers had already found him guilty before being arrested aboard the Montrose. After listening to five days of testimony, it took the jury 27 minutes to return a verdict of guilty.

Hawley Harvey Crippen stated his innocence all the way to the gallows. Pleas for clemency were denied by the Home Secretary, Winston Churchill, who, it turns out, was Crippen's eighth cousin. It went against Crippen that he didn't show remorse, which would be difficult to do if it was a crime he didn't commit. He was hanged at Pentonville Prison on a chilly Wednesday morning of November 23, 1910, just 32 days after his trial. His father, Myron, had passed away in Los Angeles four weeks earlier on October 18, blamed on the stress caused after hearing that his son was charged with murder.

Four days after Crippen's trial, Ethel Le Neve was in the dock at the Old Bailey, charged as an accessory after the fact. If Crippen had been found innocent, Ethel wouldn't have had to face the ordeal, but justice was seen to be done, and the prosecution didn't put up much of a case. The only crime she could be seen to have committed was bad taste in openly wearing Cora's clothes and jewelry, which Crippen had given her.

In the one-day trial the defense portrayed Ethel as a 17-year-old girl when she began working for Crippen and had come under his spell. Not many believed she had blindly followed his instructions, dressing as a boy under an assumed name to leave the country without asking any questions. Despite that, the jury took 12 minutes to find her not guilty.

Ethel was allowed to visit Hawley on the eve of his sentence. He had made her executor of his will, leaving her everything. However, she was barred from this as Crippen couldn't have what would have been Cora's as a murderer can't benefit from their crime.

Although Dr Crippen will never be forgot, Ethel faded from public scrutiny. She moved to Toronto, changing her name to Ethel Harvey in remembrance of her lover. She soon returned to London, acquiring a job at a furniture store where she met Stanley Smith, who she married in January 1915.

Over the years, there have been many who have revisited the case of Dr Crippen, gradually unearthing more facts. One is that on the day Winston Churchill made his decision that Crippen should hang; he received a letter claiming to be from Cora. Instead of investigating to locate the source, it was put down as being fake.

On November 13, 1910, an article appeared in the Los Angeles Herald with the report of a woman said to fit the description of Cora.

WOMAN THOUGHT TO BE BELLE ELMORE FOUND

ALIX, Alberta. Nov. 12.--Great excitement has been caused here by the report that a woman who arrived in town Wednesdy is Belle Elmore Crippen, for whose supposed death Dr. Hawley H. Crippen is under sentence to be hanged in London November 23.

After the woman alighted from the train Wednesday she went directly to a livery barn and ordered a team of horses hitched to a wagon. She left a deposit with the liveryman for the return of the team, saying she would send it back next day by a friend. The horses were returned by a farmer.

While the woman was waiting at the barn the Crippen case was being discussed by a group of men standing near her and one of them remarked : "I guess they will make old Doc Crippen sqwak over in London."

On hearing the statement the woman fainted, but soon recovered.

While in a store the woman was eagerly scanning a number of newspapers and again fainted on reading something concerning the Crippen death sentence. These occurrences, together with several of a similar nature, led to much excited speculation, especially when it was noted that her appearance tallied with the description printed of Belle Elmore. The police have the woman under surveillance and she may be arrested today.

Copy of article in Los Angeles Herald.

Arriving by train at the village of Alix in Alberta, Canada, the woman began to act very strange on learning that Dr Crippen was to be hanged.

Cora, or what was thought to be Cora's remains, was interred at Islington and Saint Pancras Cemetery with a gravestone under her stage name, Belle Elmore.

In a final letter during his incarceration, Hawley Crippen said, "I am innocent, and someday evidence will be found to prove it." It appears that he was correct, even if it doesn't change the decision of his guilt in the eyes of the law.

DNA appears to be revolutionary when proving guilt but doubted when proving innocence. When toxicologist John Trestrail decided to do some research on the historic murder, even he couldn't have

MILLER SAYS WOMAN CANNOT BE MRS. CRIPPEN

Chicago, Nov. 12.— Bruce Miller, who was witness at the trial of Dr. Crippen, and is the only man in this country, it is said, who could identify Belle Elmore, placed no credence in this report from Alberta that the woman had appeared in the town of Alix, or anywhere else, for that matter.

"Belle Elmore had no friends or relatives in that section of the country so far as I know," said Miller. "As I have said before, there is no doubt that she is dead—murdered, as was proved in court."

SAY BELLE ELMORE STORY FAKE

CALGARY, Alberta. Nov. 12.—Investigtion by the Royal Northwest mounted police shows there is no truth in the story circulated from Alix, Alberta, today that Belle Elmore, wife of Dr. Harvey H. Crippen, was there. The story, it is said, is wholly a prouct of the imagination.

Copy of article in Los Angeles Herald.

imagined the results would be so astounding. The body parts from the basement may have been buried, but samples used in the trial are still being kept at New Scotland Yard's Police Evidence Museum and the Royal London Hospital Archives and Museum, with the latter offering the forensic team at Michigan State University one of the slides.

In 2010, the case report was published with the results of years of work in chasing a paper trail for Cora's relatives. With Cora having no known children, three of her great-nieces were located who readily gave DNA samples. Though the DNA from the three females showed they were related to each other, there was no match to the sample said to be Cora. What the results did show is that the DNA belongs to a male.

Did Cora's friends believe her husband had murdered her and without a body would get away with it? They certainly had influential friends who pushed Scotland Yard to make further investigations after Inspector Dew's visit. It's not improbable for someone to have planted the evidence, as in March, Crippen and Le Never were vacationing in France. Any of Cora's friends could have known someone who worked at an asylum where the deceased often ended up as pathological specimens. It didn't require a whole body to find someone guilty of murder, and it would explain the presence of hyoscine, if that's what it was, which was widely being used on mental patients. It's also strange that Cora's comb and curlers containing her hair were placed in the grave.

Later investigations found that Cora's sister, Tessa Hunn, who was a witness at Crippen's trial, had a singer named Belle Rose living with her. Belle Rose had arrived in New York from Bermuda and also fit the description of Cora Crippen.

The team of scientists informed the UK government of their findings, looking to reopen the case. In 2009 the criminal cases review commission decided not to reopen the case. Crippen's son, Hawley Otto Crippen, died on January 30, 1974, at 85-years-old. Being married twice, he had no known surviving children. A more distant relative wrote to prime Minister Boris Johnson, asking for his ancestor's remains and a pardon so Dr Crippen can be returned to America for reburial. Unfortunately, only direct descendants have the

right to make a claim but bearing the name James Patrick Crippen has
been a burden.

THE ENFIELD POLTERGEIST

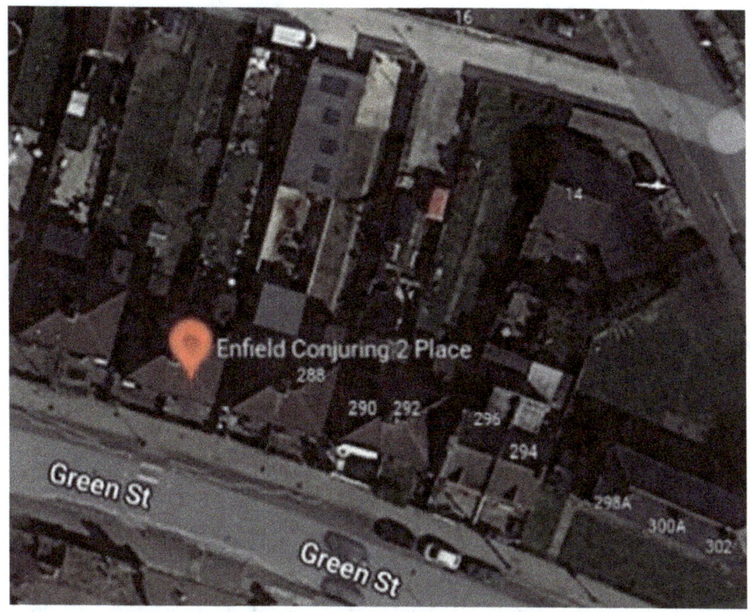

Imagery copyright 2022 Bluesky, Getmapping plc

The most famous case of a haunted house is in Amityville, much to the annoyance of the town's residents. The book, but more the film, has kept it alive with its sequels that still attract sightseers.

Then there is the Sallie House at Atchison in Kansas and what has become known as The Conjuring House at Harrisville, Rhode Island. Both of which claim the paranormal phenomena still exists.

Some hauntings are permanent, while others continue for a short period or until the family moves on. In the case known as the Enfield Poltergeist, the activity appeared to calm down.

Peggy Hodgson, a single mother with four children, Margaret (13), Janet (11), Johnny (10) and Billy (7), lived in a rented semi-detached council house at 284 Green Street in Brimsdown, Enfield, Greater London.

On the evening of August 30, 1977, the girls were being so noisy that Peggy shouted at them to go to sleep. The girls told her it wasn't them, so she went upstairs to see what was happening. And what was happening was frightening. Peggy saw a heavy oak chest of drawers move across the room. Appearing to be heading for the door to trap them in the bedroom, Peggy gathered all the kids and told them to get out of the house, taking them to a neighbor.

When Peggy told her neighbour's, Vic and Peggy Nottingham what had happened, Vic offered to check it out. He claimed that on entering the house he heard knocking on the walls and ceiling, which he found quite frightening.

Peggy then called the police, hoping they could help. Police Constable Carolyn Heep, who attended the call, very bravely made a statement of what she witnessed in the Hodgson home, which could have affected her career.

PC Heep stated that she heard taps on the walls. Then the elder son, Johnny, pointed to an armchair that had begun to wobble. It then moved around 4 feet across the floor. When it stopped, she checked the chair but couldn't find any reason for how it had moved.

An accompanying police officer checked the house, including the attic but found no one. He couldn't find any problems with any of the pipes and, with no evidence of a crime being committed, was unable to help.

The council refused to rehouse the family and so the next step was to approach the newspapers. A popular tabloid newspaper, the Daily Mirror, took up the story. From there, everyone wanted to be involved, from those with an open mind to unmovable skeptics. There were those looking to witness the events at Green Street, those who wanted to prove it was a hoax and those who really wanted to help the family.

Journalists, neighbors, psychics and paranormal investigators all visited the house. They heard taps and other noises. They saw furniture move and toys being thrown. Photographs were taken of Margaret and Janet levitating, which were used by the skeptics to say they proved it was a hoax. And they could be right, as they show the girls appearing to jump in the air rather than being lifted by an invisible force.

Maurice Grosse and Guy Lyon Playfair of the Society for Psychological Research were called in by the newspaper to investigate. They saw the stress and anxiety the family were going through as things had got so bad, they were all sleeping in one room with the light on. Grosse was more affected as he had joined the society after his daughter, also named Janet, had died in a motorbike accident only the year before. He wanted to help but first had to understand what they were dealing with. Documenting the case with what was available at that time, he recorded interviews with the family on a reel-to-reel tape recorder and cameras with a timer were set up to take photographs every 15 seconds. Being the 1970s there wasn't all the ghost hunting equipment like today, and cine cameras could only film manually.

The girls did admit to faking some of the activity to see if the paranormal investigators would catch them out, which they did. Unfortunately, this gave members of the newly formed Committee for Skeptical Inquiry (CSI) ammunition to claim that all the evidence was faked. In their opinion, if there was no logical reason, then it could be nothing more than lies and deceit while believers were no more than gullible.

The family lived in a house where raps on walls and ceilings, doors opening and closing, and voices continued day and night. The comings and goings of the news media to those wanting to see the house, caused some neighbors to turn on the family. The children, more so Janet and Billy were bullied at school with nicknames such as Ghost Girl and Freak.

Peggy just wanted it to stop, never seeking publicity, and in later years refused to give any interviews. The family never made any money from their unwanted fame, and the newspapers had a good story while it lasted. Maurice Grosse used the evidence he had collected to lecture on the Enfield case and took part in documentaries as late as 2008. When Guy Lyon Playfair published "This House is Haunted: The True Story of the Enfield Poltergeist" in 1980, he was a little more skeptical, though stood by his belief that the house was haunted.

Along with those looking to visit the Enfield house was a self-proclaimed demonologist, Ed Warren and his wife Lorraine, who often went seeking out high profile cases. Playfair said they arrived uninvited and told him he could make a lot of money from the case. The Warrens certainly did. After being there for one day, they proclaimed it to be demonic and added it to their files of cases in which they had been involved. They later made money from The Amityville Horror and The Conjuring House, with "Conjuring 2" taking background from the Enfield case to make the horror movie.

Dr Melvin Willin, a member of the Psychological Society, also continues to make money from the case with "The Enfield Poltergeist Tapes: one of the most disturbing cases in history. What really happened?" published in 2019.

With the two girls being the center of the attacks, Maurice Grosse concentrated on them, especially Janet, when she began talking in a deep, gruff voice. With her lips barely moving, apart from growls, barks and whistles, the voice came out with a lot of cussing and many different names. One, however, matched a former tenant of the house. The gruff voice described how Bill Watkins died, which was verified by Bill's son.

Magicians decided that they could produce the same tricks without considering that these were children without any magic skills. Even a top British ventriloquist, Ray Alan thought Janet was using ventriloquism. An expert found that Janet was using what is called a false vocal cord above the larynx, which if used too often would cause a sore throat. Maurice Grosse claimed that Janet could talk in this manner for hours, all being recorded with no ill effects. He placed tape over her mouth and got her to drink water with no change to the voice. When the microphone was placed behind her, the continuity sounded the same. Janet said in an interview that the voice didn't feel like it was coming from her but from behind her.

It was suggested that Janet was the problem, it being widely accepted that teenagers and puberty can trigger energy that results in poltergeist type activity. And in real life and horror films, using a ouija board can also generate negative energy. The girls admitted that just before everything kicked off at Green Street, they had used a homemade ouija board.

The activity increased during the investigation, then after 18 months quietened down. This may have been after a priest was called in to bless the house. With the poltergeist no longer performing on command, the media turned to other subjects. Apart from rehashing the story, mainly in the form of television documentaries, to the sequel of the "The Conjuring" being "The Conjuring 2" movie released in 2016, it is all but forgotten.

Like the case of the Bell Witch, the activity must have become more acceptable, or Peggy just learned to live with it. She remained at the house along with Billy up to her death from breast cancer in 2003. Always having the feeling of being watched, Billy moved out.

Janet moved out at 16-years-old and got married.

Johnny was only 14 years old when he died from cancer around three years after the phenomena calmed down.

Margaret left home and married. She had a son who died in his sleep when he was 18-years-old.

After Billy moved out of 284 Green Street, a single mother with four sons moved in. The boys claimed they heard voices, and when one saw a man entering his bedroom and then finding out it was the poltergeist house, was the last straw. The family moved out after two months.

Maurice Grosse continued returning to the case, making a documentary including an interview with Margaret and Janet, now no longer girls. He died in 2006 at the age of 87.

At the time of printing, the house was sold in 2016, with the owners being adamant that it isn't haunted. However, they still have people knocking on the door, filming the house and taking pictures. It probably doesn't help that Google have labeled it on their maps.

THE FLORIDA SKUNK APE

Florida Skunk Ape. Artwork Diane Browne
copyright 2022.

Though the Skunk Ape is used as a symbol to attract tourists to the Everglades, it's widely believed to be no more than an urban legend, perpetrated by hoaxers. The Skunk Ape is said to live in the swampy lands of the Everglades that make up one and a half million acres where there is more than enough real scary species in the form of alligators, snakes, brown bears and spiders.

Also known as the Swamp Ape, it's described to be similar to Bigfoot found further north. The Skunk Ape appears in Seminole Native Indian myth with stories of a man-like ape raiding the tribe's food stores.

Sightings were prominent in the 1960s and 70s leading to a proposal in 1977 to keep it safe like Bigfoot in that no one is allowed to harm or kill one of them, even with no solid proof of their existence.

The Skunk Ape walks on two legs with a similar body to Bigfoot but differing in size, being slightly smaller in height between 5-7 feet. Its hair is a more reddish color, but most distinctive is the smell, described as being like skunk spray.

Some people spend all their spare time hunting for the Skunk Ape, producing casts of large footprints, grainy photographs and film footage. In 1997 around 30 people on a bus taking a tour of the Everglades reservation all claimed to have seen an animal resembling the creature. Another man claimed that a Skunk Ape ran out in front of his car, managing to take a picture just before it disappeared from sight.

The Seminole and Miccosukee tribes that were prominent in Florida passed down the stories over the centuries about the Skunk Ape, which is thought to have gotten the name in the 1960s.

According to an article on the Smithsonian website, Dan Shealy, founder of the Skunk Ape Research Headquarters in Ochopee, Florida, claims to have had several sightings since he was 10-years-old. The research center caters to tourists running boat trips and buggy rides in the swamplands. There is also a gift shop.

Government warning sign. Photograph by Joseph Stromberg.

Scientists believe that reported Skunk Ape sightings are more likely misidentified, such as deer or bear. However, there is more than one primate breeding center in the area. One is near Immokalee in Collier County having strict warning signs.

FORETELLING OF THE TITANIC

Titanic during sea trials photographed by Francis Godolphin Osbourne Stuart.

One of the world's most famous ships is best known for all the wrong reasons. It was advertised as the biggest and best. Taking inspiration from Greek mythology for what was to be the largest ship of its day, the Titanic was built in the dockyards at Belfast in Ireland. Its sister ship, the Olympic, was already in service but had suffered several problems, that it ended up in the next dock for repairs, using some of the parts made for the Titanic. Due to this, it later brought about conspiracy theories that the ships were swapped.

The White Star Line needed Titanic to do what she was built for, being above the luxury of any high-class hotel, and for speed. They also had to better their competitors, Cunard, who had the fastest ships, Lusitania and Mauritania.

Taking over two years to build, the Olympic was begun first and the Titanic three months later. Changes to the Titanic were made during its building, making rooms bigger and changing the windows in first class.

Titanic undertook a sea trial on April 2, 1912, which took around

12 hours. On returning to Belfast, the surveyor signed her off as seaworthy. Registering its home port as Liverpool, where most of the liners sailed from, it was more convenient for passengers from London to sail from Southampton.

With some of the fitments and fixings not being completed in the second and third-class, Titanic set sail from Southampton on April 10, 1912. The largest contingency was third-class, who was the first to board. Second class passengers were shown to their cabins by stewards while the opulent first-class were greeted by the captain, Edward John Smith, who had been sequestered from the Olympic.

On leaving the dock, the swell from such a large ship caused two others to rise so high that the New York broke its moorings, missing a collision by 4 feet. The departure was delayed by an hour while waiting for a tugboat to tow the New York to a safe distance.

Four hours later, the Titanic dropped anchor off Cherbourg, where there wasn't a suitable dock for such a Titan of a ship. Two boats were provided by the White Star Line to ferry 274 passengers to the Titanic and 24 passengers who disembarked.

On April 11, the same method was used to ferry 123 passengers from the docks at Queenstown (now Cobh) in Ireland and disembarked 7 people, including Father Francis Browne who took many photographs while on board.

Titanic then began its journey to New York, where she was expected to dock on April 17th. It's said that the chairman of the White Star Line, Joseph Bruce Ismay, who was also aboard, was pushing the captain to go faster to break the speed record. It would have been a feather in 62-year-old Captain Smith's cap as he was coming up for retirement.

Fires often broke out in the bunkers due to heat from the furnaces. Such a fire had broken out on the Titanic and had been smoldering for days before the voyage. Apart from this and the near-miss with the New York, everything appeared to be going smoothly.

Other ships in the area sent out warnings of icebergs but these weren't considered to be a problem for larger ships, especially the Titanic. Up to this time, icebergs had caused damage but with no loss of lives. And as usual, there were crewmembers on the lookout who would report any sightings.

On the evening of the 14th, William Murdoch, the ship's first officer, was on duty when Frederick Fleet, one of two lookouts in the tower above, reported an iceberg dead ahead. Murdoch ordered the ship to reverse and turn away, which would take time and even longer with going at high speed. The warning had come too late, and the Titanic scraped its side against the iceberg like a car hitting a gate post. For such a large ship, the damage should have been minimal and easy to control. The dent caused a tear, and the ship began to fill with water, making the front dip down and the rear to rise so high that the propellers could be seen. Once the front went below the cold icy water, it rushed into the decks below, eventually pulling the vessel beneath the waves.

The original date for the Titanic's maiden voyage, set for March, was delayed that everything was done in a rush to get the ship underway. Within two hours of hitting the iceberg it was obvious the ship was not going to survive. The crew hadn't had any emergency drills, and then there was the lifeboats. It was designed to take 64 wooden lifeboats apart from several collapsible boats that in total would accommodate over 4000 people. Only 14 wooden and 4 collapsible boats that would safely take around 900 at the side of 1,425 passengers and crew had been fitted. The lifeboats would have been sufficient for all 534 women and children, but most were lowered half full. At the hearings that followed, the passenger list was difficult to sort out as some tickets were cancelled, and one crew member had slipped off the ship at Queenstown.

The Titanic's demise was originally fiction that turned into reality at least twice. There were many fictional stories of sinking ships, except for two publications that could be a prequel to the Titanic.

William Thomas Stead had his short story "How the Mail Steamer Went Down

W. T. Stead.

in Mid Atlantic, by a Survivor" published in the Pall Mall Gazette issued on March 22, 1886. Stead wasn't just an author of fiction but began his career as a journalist, becoming the youngest editor in Britain at 22-years-old.

The story, being a narration of a serving crew member, is about an unnamed ship that took mail and passengers. And like the Titanic, it sailed from Queenstown. Being shrouded in fog and like the Titanic, having limited vision, it wasn't an iceberg but a smaller ship that crossed the mail steamer's path. Like the Titanic, there weren't enough lifeboats. In a desperate panic, some were dropped without being full as some of the crew mutinied to save themselves. Stead, being the Gazette's editor, added an endnote that the story might and will take place if liners are sent to sea with a shortage of lifeboats.

Ironically, W. T. Stead was a passenger on the Titanic, being one of the 1,514 who lost their lives. His body was never recovered, so didn't get to see the Montrose rescue survivors. He did write another story, "From the Old World to the New World," published in 1892, where a ship named the Majestic rescued The Ann and Jane of Montrose after hitting an iceberg.

A novel more often cited as foretelling the sinking of the Titanic is "Futility" by Morgan Robertson, published in 1898. It was revised in 1912, adding the extra title of "The Wreck of the Titan."

Morgan Robertson.

Morgan Andrew Robertson was an American author of short stories and novels, many being sea tales. His love of the sea came from his father, a ship's captain who traversed the Great Lakes, taking Morgan with him during school holidays.

Giving his fated ship the name "Titan" is so close to the real fated "Titanic." Both ships were British made. The two ships were similar in size, with both having three propellers. The Titan had a few more passengers, but both had fewer lifeboats than needed. Both Titan and Titanic set sail on their maiden voyage in April, and both hit an iceberg at around the same time of 11.40pm in the North Atlantic just off Newfoundland.

Though Robertson's stories were popular in his day, all but Futility have fallen into obscurity, becoming even more popular after the Titanic disaster.

People now wonder if Robertson was psychic, giving him the ability to see future events. His story, published in 1914, "Beyond the Spectrum," describes a sneak attack by Japan on the United States. The sneak attack by the Japanese on Pearl Harbor took place on December 7, 1941.

The prolific writer was staying at the Almanac Hotel in Atlantic City, New Jersey, when on March 24, 1915, he was found dead. Some years before, he complained that he had made little money from his writing, and then his story was linked to the Titanic disaster. Though it brought extra sales, it must have been depressing. At 53-years-old Morgan Robertson was found to have died from an overdose of paraldehyde.

THE MARY CELESTE

"Amazon of Parrsboro" 1861, later renamed "Mary Celeste" author unknown.

The oceans of the world continue to hold many mysteries, from monsters on old maps to fish washing up on shorelines that were thought to have been long extinct. When man took to the water, building boats for trade, exploration and war, it brought more mysteries, haunted ships and conspiracies.

One of these is the Mary Celeste which had somewhat of a past. On its launch in 1861, it was given the name Amazon. She was built in Nova Scotia, Canada, sailing for seven years under the Union Jack. From its maiden voyage, disaster struck. Carrying timber, the Amazon set sail for London only for Captain Robert McLellan to fall ill. The ship returned to Nova Scotia, where he died.

John Nutting Parker became her new captain, and the ship set sail once again. This was also not without its problems, as just off Maine, the Amazon became entangled in fishing nets. She finally reached London, but tragedy struck once again when there was a collision with one of the many masted brigs in the English Channel.

Captain Parker remained at the helm until 1863, when William Thompson became Amazon's new captain, sailing trade routes around the West Indies and English ports. Captain Thompson had been in command for four years when a storm blew the ship onto the shore of Cape Breton Island, Nova Scotia, where it was abandoned as a wreck. Several days later, it was sold to Alexander McBean, who quickly sold it on to New York businessman Richard Haines, who set about making it seaworthy. Fancying himself as a seaman, he became captain of the newly named Mary Celeste, not the French-sounding Marie. Registering the ship in America, she now sailed under the stars and stripes. Unfortunately, Haines's fortune ran out, and the Mary Celeste was taken by his creditors. It was then sold to a consortium, which over the years changed members but remained in the hands of the majority stockholder, James Winchester. Around this time, not much is known about the Mary Celeste, as no records have been found. She could have been used for leisure or even darker means such as gun running. Before the 1873 stock market crash, the Mary Celeste was given an overhaul, adding a second deck and extending her length, width and depth.

Benjamin Spooner Briggs, a member of the consortium became her captain and prepared for its first voyage since the refit. Apart from a crew of seven men, Captain Briggs' wife Sarah and their 2-year-old daughter Matilda joined them. Arthur, their 7-year-old son, had to attend school and was dispatched to his grandparents.

With a cargo of 1700 barrels of industrial alcohol, the Mary Celeste set sail from New York on November 5, 1872. But due to reports of bad weather, they anchored off Staten Island.

Two days later, on the 7th, the ship began its journey to Genoa, Italy.

On November 15, the Del Gratia set sail for Gibraltar, then on to Genoa. Nineteen days into the voyage, a ship was spotted between the Azores and receiving no reply to their signals, the first mate and a crew member were sent over to the ship. Getting closer, they could see it was the Mary Celeste. Once aboard, they found no signs of life. A few personal items were moving with the list of the ship and there was a broken compass. A couple of hatches had been left open, allowing water to get into the hold, but the cargo looked to be untouched. The lifeboat was missing, and apart from damage to the sails and water entering through open doors and skylights, the ship was in good condition. The last entry in the ship's log was dated November 25 at 8.00am, reporting its position around 400 miles from where it was found.

Captain Morehouse knew there was money to be made from the salvage. By law, he could receive half the ship's value and its cargo. Dividing his crew of seven men, the Del Gratia returned to Gibraltar, arriving two days before the Mary Celeste. The abandoned ship was quickly seized by the vice Admiralty to examine it for a court hearing.

The court convened four days later, hearing that cuts had been found on the hull, though there had been no collision. A sword belonging to Captain Briggs was said to have blood on the blade, and red stains on a railing were also thought to be fragments of blood, which were sent to be tested. Despite the cargo of alcohol being poisonous, and no barrels having been disturbed, the popular belief was that the crew had got drunk and mutinied. Putting together a report containing such claims, Frederick Solly-Flood, the Attorney General of Gibraltar helped to create the mystery of the Mary Celeste. He then came up with two more theories to what could have happened. With no reports of bad weather, he couldn't believe an unmanned ship would have sailed so far. In his scenario, he had Captain Briggs and Captain Morehouse in cahoots, plotting to claim the salvage. He was sure the captain and crew of the Del Gratia weren't telling everything they knew. Another theory was that James Winchester, the largest shareholder, had hired the crew to kill Captain Briggs and his family. This fell flat when the claimed bloodstains were later revealed to be rust.

The Mary Celeste was released from Gibraltar and sailed to Italy to deliver its cargo. However, the stories of the ship were already being printed in newspapers, with wild stories, from pirates boarding and killing the crew to accusing Captain Briggs of killing his family during a manic episode.

With its reputation and stories of the mystery expanding, 15-months later, the consortium sold the Mary Celeste at a loss. She went on to sail around the West Indies between the islands and the mainland, then the captain, Edgar Tuthill, fell ill and docked at Saint

Helena, seeking medical help. When Captain Tuthill died on the island, it confirmed to some that the ship was cursed.

Her last voyage bound for Tahiti was in 1884, with a cargo of goods insured for $30,000. As planned with the owners, Captain Gilman Parker deliberately ran her onto a reef known for its many shipwrecks. Of course, it was an insurance scam with the cargo being worthless. An investigation quickly found the fraud, and the captain was charged with conspiracy. The trial resulted in a hung jury, but rather than having a retrial, which could have meant a death sentence for the captain, a deal was made where all the money from the salvage was repaid. It left Gilman Parker's reputation in tatters, and shortly after he died in poverty.

Whatever happened to Captain Briggs, his family and crew, if he had entered into the log the reason the lifeboat was lowered, there would be no mystery. Stories involve pirates, mutiny, alien abduction, conspiracy and murder, to the captain being defamed with him looking to start a new life. After 150 years with only theories, it's impossible to solve the mystery absolutely.

Today, on the shore of Spencer Island sits a memorial to the Mary Celeste and her lonesome voyage, along with the ten people that were never seen or heard from again.

Memorial to the lost crew of the Mary Celeste. Spencer's Island, Nova Scotia, Canada. Lost at Sea.

MERMAIDS

Tales of mermaids are worldwide, going back centuries. Hans Christian Andersen's story "The Little Mermaid" inspired the statue that sits in the arbor in Copenhagen. Being commissioned by Carl Jacobsen, the son and heir to the Carlsberg Brewery, the bronze and granite statue was then gifted to his home town. The Mermaid sat on her granite rock, looking towards the shore in the hope of seeing the man she fell in love with, had an unveiling ceremony on August 23, 1913. Carl Jacobsen was not only inspired by Hans Christian Andersen but a ballet based on the fairytale performed at the Royal Danish Theater. Ellen Price, the ballerina playing the mermaid, was asked to pose for the

Painting by John William Waterhouse 1900.

sculptor, Edvard Eriksen, who for some reason, required her to be nude. Ellen refused, and so the likeness is of Eriksen's wife, Eline.

Unfortunately, the times we live in means that iconic artwork such as the Little Mermaid is a target for vandalism, with the head being decapitated and stolen, it is not the original. After several other attacks just for the hell of it to political statements, security cameras now watch over her.

Some mermaid sightings describe webbed fingers, either with short stumpy arms or long slender limbs. The hair is usually long, being blond to black and even green. The descriptions range from a beautiful face to large and round, and even a cross between animal and human features.

The Greek sirens were part fish and part bird with colorful feathers, but over the ages came to blend in to become more like merpeople with a fishtail and human body.

In Chinese legends, merpeople date back to the 4th century BC, being called shark people. And if real mermaids and mermen can't be found, there are those who enjoy the fast-growing trend of mermaiding. The underwater displays of merfolk can lead to a prominent career. Ripley's Believe it or Not, mermaid shows provide entertainment around the world. China holds an annual competition attracting like-minded people from all over the world and there are also mermaiding courses. In 2021, at the Atlantis Sanya Sea Resort, 110 mermaid divers completed a choreographed underwater show to get into the Guinness Book of Records.

Mermaiding from Pixabay.

PT Barnum produced a real-life Tom Thumb in the form of Charles Stratton, but his Fiji mermaid, first put on display in London in 1822, was a mummified specimen and not the depicted beautiful creatures of legend, being the bottom half of a fish sewn onto the top half of a young monkey.

In Celtic legend, merfolk, known as Selkies, are said to be friendly creatures who live in water. There are also mermen, who seem to be more elusive, or may just be less curious about humans. Legends of merpeople don't just belong to the seas and oceans but pools and lakes with stories of those having drowned by accident or suicide turning into merpeople.

In 1809, several newspapers, the first being the Kentish Gazette, reported the sighting of a mermaid at Thurso in Caithness, Scotland. Two young ladies were taking a walk along the shore at Sandside Bay when they came upon three people standing on a rock looking into the sea. They soon found what was taking their attention. A mermaid, no more than a few yards away, seemed somewhat annoyed as each wave pushed the long hair over her face. The five people watched for over an hour, giving the ladies a chance to describe the creature in some detail. They wrote a letter of their encounter describing a large round face, small nose, small grey eyes and large mouth. The arms and fingers were slender but not webbed as in some descriptions. After the article was published, a schoolmaster wrote a letter to the Kentish Gazette. He claimed to have seen what he at first thought was a naked woman sitting on a rock combing her long brown hair at the same location 12-years earlier. His description was similar to the two ladies, except his mermaid had blue eyes. He watched for several minutes before the mermaid became aware of his presence and, plunging into the sea, disappeared into its depths. Over the years prior to the schoolmaster and the two ladies' encounters, there had been numerous sightings. The newspaper caused a stir, which like all other sightings, soon dwindled when there were no more reports.

Durham Castle's Chapel in England has many carvings, including mermaids. Being built around 1080, 14-years into the reign of William the Conqueror, Durham Castle was one of many fortresses across the country to fend off any other invaders. At the time, depicting mermaids in church architecture would have represented temptation.

Sailors talked of mermaids singing to them in an attempt to lure the crew to their palace at the bottom of the sea. The famous pirate Blackbeard, mainly attacked and plundered French and Spanish ships around the Indian Ocean and Caribbean in the early 18th century. And, like many at the time, was superstitious. In his ship's log, Captain Blackbeard made entries of places he avoided, calling them "enchanted" where merfolk had been sighted. An encounter with a mermaid was an ill omen and could lose them their plunder as the merpeople would drag it to the bottom of the sea.

A very realistic mermaid washed up on a Mexican Beach in 2014, which turned out to be a model for the film "Pirates of the Caribbean." During filming in 2011, the movie had to take a break during a storm and the mermaid was washed out to sea.

Christopher Columbus spent years at sea, so it should be no surprise that he claimed to have had his own sighting. His description of the three beings seen off the shores of Hispaniola disappointed him as they weren't the beauties that legend proclaimed. It is now thought his merpeople, like many other sightings, were manatees, now an endangered species.

Trichechus manatus latirostris underwater manatee by author Jim P. Retd. U.S. Fish and Widlife Service.

The British explorer and navigator Henry Hudson, also had his own tale to tell. While on an expedition in 1608 to find a trade route to China via the Arctic Circle, Hudson and the ship's crew reported seeing a mermaid in the Arctic. The creature was evidently curious as it came close to the ship, being described as a naked female. But when she swam back into the depths, they saw a tail like a porpoise. Maybe the sighting was an ill omen as the northeast passage remained elusive until 1878, when it was successfully completed by a Swedish expedition.

In 1611, Henry Hudson, in his continuing quest to find the route to Asia, took the decision to explore what is now known as Hudson Bay. With the onset of winter, Hudson's new ship, Discovery, was trapped in ice with the crew seeking shelter on land. Once it became obvious that it wasn't the trade route, and having been at sea for two years, the crew wanted to head for home. The only record of the incident was by the ship's navigator, Abacuk Pricket, who kept a journal that is dubious at best.

Henry Hudson was busy charting the shoreline and had no intention of turning back. The crew became more restless, eventually turning to mutiny. Pricket's testimony, and those of the surviving mutineers, claimed they set Henry Hudson, his son, John and seven of the crew suffering from scurvy into a small boat used for coastal navigation. Whatever the true story, Henry Hudson, his son, nor the crewmen were ever seen again.

There have always been stories of mermaids around the shores of Israel. When a promenade was built for people to walk along the coastline at the resort of Kiryat Yam, around 2008, both locals and tourists began reporting mermaid sightings around Haifa Bay. Some just watched while others filmed, posting the clips on social media. This prompted Schmuel Sisso, the town's mayor, to put up a reward of one million dollars for "unbreakable proof" of the mermaids' existence. Shortly after the reward was announced, the mayor received a letter threatening to take him to the International Court of Justice for endangering the mermaid by encouraging people to try and capture the creature. In 2009 an NBC news crew filmed along the beach for a week and caught a few seconds of some creature that couldn't be identified. Divers were sent down but couldn't locate anything resembling what was on the film. Whether a hoax or not, the resort benefitted as tourism grew.

That wasn't the first reward offered. In 1967 a ferry carrying tourists near British Columbia's Mayne islands claimed to have seen a blonde-haired mermaid languishing on the beach eating a salmon. A second sighting produced a picture that prompted Charlie White to offer a reward of $25,000 for the capture of the creature. Charlie, who died in 2010, was an author on fishing and marine life as well as a television celebrity. Being the founder of "Undersea Gardens" with many marine exhibits, he presumably hoped to have a mermaid on show. The story and sightings soon fizzled out.

Every decade seems to have a breaking story of a mermaid somewhere in the world, with no one has yet, proving that merfolk are no more than a race of lost people, or if they have always been just a fairytail.

THE POOKA

Pooka horse. Artwork Diane Browne copyright 2022.

The Pooka is rooted in Irish mythology. If you've seen the 1950 film "Harvey" starring James Stewart, you will have an idea of what a Pooka can do.

Harvey is a rabbit that only James Stewart's character can see, a Pooka is a goblin, fairy or shapeshifter that can take the form of a human or animal and is often associated with the devil.

However, in some parts of Ireland, a Pooka is supposed to be a good spirit, making an appearance to help or warn of some unforeseen doom.

Unlike Halloween being one night each year, in olden times, a Pooka held power throughout November with the ability to make prophecies. At Easter, it was thought to be the Easter Bunny.

The Pooka influenced poems and stories, including William Shakespeare with his character Puck, a magical elf in "A Midsummer Night's Dream."

The following is an amended version of a short story by Patrick Kennedy (1801-1873) published in 1866.

* * *

THE KILDARE POOKA

The master of the manor house in County Kildare, Ireland, spent little time there. He was either away on business or spending time at his other home in Dublin.

The retained servants continued to keep the house as though the family was in residence. At the end of each day, a stable boy would get to what heat he could from the fire as the servants sat around the kitchen's hearth chattering and telling ghost stories. The stable boy would return to the barn, and the servants went to their beds for another restless night's sleep. As when everyone was in bed, they would wake to the sounds of doors slamming and pots and pans clattering. No one was brave enough to go downstairs to investigate.

One night the boy had curled up by the fire and fallen asleep. He was suddenly awoken by the door being opened, bringing in a cold blast of wind.

Apart from the embers burning in the hearth, the room was in darkness. However, he could make out a big ass standing before the fire on its hind legs. The animal snorted at the boy who wanted to call out, but nothing came from him. His fear turned to surprise as the ass spoke.

"I may as well begin," said the ass and went back outside. It soon returned with a bucket of water drawn from the well. Stoking up the fire, a cauldron was set over the flames, and the water poured in with the boy thinking he would be next in the pot.

Instead, the ass took all the cutlery and placed it in the water, then all the plates and crockery. The boy pretended to be asleep as he peeped through narrowed eyes to watch the ass scrub the table and chairs and sweep the floor so clean the master could have eaten from it. The pots and cutlery were all washed and neatly put back in place.

Without another word, the ass opened the door slamming it so hard behind him that the boy felt the house shake.

The next morning the boy told the servants what he had seen. They now knew all the noises they heard were from this creature which they all agreed was a Pooka, washing the pots and cleaning the kitchen. It was the only thing they talked about all that day, and then, a rather lazy scullery maid voiced the obvious.

"If the Pooka is doing all the cleaning up, why are we slaving away?"

They all agreed with her wise words and that night went to bed without a plate or a dish seeing a drop of water. The next morning everything was fine as fine. And so, the servants had an easy time, leaving the kitchen for the Pooka to clean.

This went on for some nights until the stable boy said he would stay up the night and talk to the Pooka. He was a little daunted when the door was thrown open, and the ass marched up to the fire.

"Sir," says the boy, picking up courage. "if it isn't taking a liberty, might I ask who you are and why you do the servant's work each night?"

"No liberty at all," says the Pooka. "I'll tell you, and welcome, I was a servant to the present lord's father. I was the laziest rogue that was ever clothed and fed, doing nothing for it. When my time came for the other world, the punishment was laid on me to come here and do all the labor every night, and then go out in the cold. It isn't so bad in fine weather, but if you only knew what it is to stand with your head between your legs, facing the storm, from midnight to sunrise, on a bleak winter night."

The boy took pity on the Pooka. "Is there anything we can do for your comfort?"

"I don't know," says the Pooka. "Maybe a good quilted frieze coat would take off the chill."

"We would be most ungrateful people if we can't repay you for your work," the boy replied.

The boy told the others what the Pooka had said, and soon they had put together a coat to fit the asses back and legs. And that night, the boy waited for the Pooka to give him the gift.

Helping to put the coat on the Pooka and buttoning it up along his belly, he was so pleased.

"I am much obliged to you and your fellow servants," the ass told the boy. "You have made me happy at last." The Pooka turned to the door. "Good night to you."

"You're going too soon," the boy reminded him. "What about the washing and sweeping?"

"Ah, you may tell the girls they must now get their turn. My punishment was to last till I was thought worthy of a reward for doing my duty. You'll see me no more." And no more they did, and right sorry they were for having been in such a hurry to reward the ungrateful Pooka.

* * *

In the 10th century, a King of Ireland, Brian Boru, went into legend when, with a magic bridle, he captured a Pooka in the form of a horse, riding it to exhaustion until it surrendered. The King told the Pooka he would release it if firstly, it would promise not to bother Christians and stop ruining their property. The Pooka also agreed not to attack an Irishman unless they were abroad on evil doings or drunk. Hence many a drunken Irishman has claimed to have been overpowered by a Pooka.

A Pooka enjoys mayhem and suffering. If the hens stop laying, cows stop giving milk, and crops don't grow, it's easy to blame a Pooka.

Many countries have legends of their own Pooka and shapeshifters. Ireland has many, the best known being the Leprechaun.

A Pooka is believed to be more mischievous than evil, though dangerous in being responsible for illness and wrecking ships off the Irish coast.

Recognizing a Pooka is by the eyes, which either will be glowing red, be a gold color or said to glitter like metal. No matter what the shape, a Pooka has the ability to talk. At one time, on the last Sunday of July, known as Bilberry Sunday, Irish folk in County Fermanagh would go to Binlaughlin Mountain and wait for the Pooka to appear in the form of a horse in the hope of receiving advice or have their fortune told.

Showing respect to a Pooka will earn respect.

The Pooka live on hillsides, in caves, forests, and water like a nature spirit. By the River Liffey there is what is called "The Pooka Hole."

At Belco in County Fermanagh, before Christians arrived and ran out the druids, what is now St. Patrick's Wells were called Pooka Pools. However, the pagan ways continue to integrate into Christian prayer with pilgrimages to worship the sun, the water and the stones. There is an annual event that takes place in August. What was once a Pooka Pool is now a place of healing, particularly for nervous disorders and stomach problems.

QUEEN ANNE'S STATUE

Queen Anne statue. Artwork Diane Browne copyright 2022.

A statue standing on a plinth can be found at Queen Anne's Gate in Westminster, London. The statue is of Queen Anne, the daughter of the deposed King James II of Great Britain.

Though she died young at the age of 49, Queen Anne was pregnant 17 times throughout her 25-year marriage to Prince George of Denmark with no surviving issue. This led to the queen being the last monarch of the House of Stuart. Though James had children while in exile, they were catholic, so the government offered the nearest non-Catholic relative the crown, being George I of Hanover.

Anne was popular with the statue depicting her at a young age as she gained weight in the later years of her reign.

Becoming queen on her brother-in-law's death in 1702 until 1714, the statue was originally set in the middle of the road at the junction of Queens Square, leading onto Park Street. Though the sculptor's name is long lost, it is thought to have been erected around 1708.

In 1874, the road was narrowed and merged to become Queen Anne's Gate. This was probably due to the statue being removed in 1814 and placed where it can be found today, between houses 15 and 13. At this time, the queen had lost her nose and right arm due to vandalism. Becoming discolored and the inscription being lost under the grime-ridden city, children thought the statue was Mary I, the eldest daughter of Henry VIII who continues to be reviled with the name "Bloody Mary." Children would call out to the statue to come down from its pedestal, and when she didn't move, would throw stones. The only remembrances remaining of Mary I are portraits, some of her clothes and documents such as letters and housekeeping records.

Residents complained about the condition of the statue, leading to a dispute over ownership. A plaster cast of the nose was made, and the right arm replaced with one of marble, the rest of the statue and its plinth being of portland stone quarried on the Isle of Portland, Dorset.

During WW2, a wall was built around the statue to protect it during air raids and wasn't removed until 1947, two years after the war ended. And it wasn't until February 1970 that it was listed as a Grade 1 statue, which means it is now maintained by Historic England.

The statue is said to come alive and though the pedestal is very high, steps down to walk around the streets of Queen Anne's Gate. This is said to take place once a year on August 1st, the date of Queen Anne's death.

The queen doesn't seem to have much luck with her statues. There is a more regal commemoration of her in the forecourt of St. Paul's Cathedral, though this is not an exact replica of the original that once stood there.

When Christopher Wren's cathedral was finished, Anne had been the monarch for 6-years. The queen provided the marble for a statue of herself that was unveiled in a ceremony in July 1713, just over a year before her death. The statue was attacked during the reigns of George II, George III and Queen Victoria, damaging her arms and nose that eventually led to weather damage.

The statue and plinth that stands in the forecourt today was commissioned in 1885, which this time was paid for by the people of London by way of taxes.

The original was later found in a stonemason's yard and bought by author Augustus Hare, who had it installed in the grounds of his house at Holmhurst St. Mary, near Hastings. Since then, the house has been a school and convent until it was renovated and made into private living accommodations. The statue is still there, for now, being in a worse state from vandalism.

SAINT FRANCIS OF ASSISI

Many people will have heard of Francis of Assisi. But for those who haven't, he is the patron saint of Italy, animals and ecology.

Giovanni di Pietro di Bernardone was born in Italy around the 1180s to a cloth merchant father and a French mother. He was later renamed Francesco by his father, being shortened to Francis.

Like young people today, Francis hung out with friends from similar wealthy families, keeping up with the latest fashion trends, enjoying the pleasures of music, sport and partying.

St. Francis of Assisi. Artwork Malgotzata Wrocjna.

When Perugia, an independent region within Italy, attacked Assisi, 20-year-old Francis joined the military. He soon found that he wasn't a warrior, being captured early on. Francis was held prisoner for a year until his father paid the ransom. It's believed that during his confinement in a dark, dank cell, he began to have visions. He was also lucky to survive when suffering a bout of malaria.

He returned to his old life but wasn't the same man and two years later joined Walter III, Count of Brienne, who had formed an army to fight for his wife, Princess Elvira's inheritance and proclaim himself King of Sicily. But this wasn't to be, as a clandestine group of enemy troops infiltrated the camp, attacked William's tent and stabbed him to death.

Having another vision, Francis returned to Assisi before setting off on a pilgrimage. He hadn't gone far when he stopped off at a ruined church to pray and claimed to have had a vision of Jesus who said to him, "Francis, Francis, go and repair My house, which you can see, is falling into ruin." Looking around the chapel, Francis took it to mean that he was to repair it. Unfortunately, the only way he knew how to go about it was through his father.

Francis took some cloth from his father's business, sold it and took the money to the priest at the chapel of San Damiano to pay for the repairs. Finding out how Francis had acquired the money, he refused to take it. His father was just as angry that his son should steal from him, and after a beating, Francis was locked up in a small room. He finally escaped when his mother unlocked the door and let him out.

He wasn't put off by the quest given him and began begging for stones to restore the church. Carrying the stones and placing them himself, after two years the chapel was restored. But he didn't stop there, repairing other churches around the area of Assisi.

Choosing a solitary life, Francis lived in the hills, though stayed near Assisi. He took to wearing a tunic of sackcloth tied at the waist by a rope. He began preaching and even nursed lepers without fear of catching the disfiguring disease.

He soon attracted a following, calling those who joined him, friars. Still a young man in his mid-twenties, he travelled to Rome with eleven of his followers to ask Pope Innocent III for permission to found a religious order. Though he thought the church was too military, his work needed to be recognized by the church. The Pope gave his informal agreement and said if his following increased, Francis was to return and receive full recognition. The Pope's councilors thought Francis was no more than a young man with a dream, if not insane. But within months, the Franciscan Order became official, with a women's order also being founded.

During the fifth Holy Crusade, Francis travelled to Egypt, where he was granted an audience with the Sultan, Al-Kamil. Francis was said to have been allowed to preach but made no converts. Preaching love and peace as a Christian must have been hollow words to their ears with an army in the name of Christianity ready to fight.

Within ten years the Franciscan order had grown radically,

spreading to other countries. Unfortunately for Francis, this brought the unwanted attention of the authorities and the church, who wanted to take control and enforce their own rules. No longer being the religious order Francis had envisaged, he handed over the leadership to become a friar and continue his wanderings as a beggar. He refused to be ordained as a priest but reluctantly became a deacon. This gave him a license to preach so he wouldn't be arrested as a heretic.

In his early 40s, while Francis was praying at La Verna, set on Mount Penna in Italy, he was visited by an angel. He gave the first-ever description of an angel having wings, with artists continuing to portray these angelic beings with dove-like wings. Francis also prayed to receive and was given what is called the stigmata, the wounds Jesus received at the crucifixion. This ocurred regularly throughout the rest of his life.

His hands and feet would develop wounds as though they had been drilled through with nails. A gash would appear on his side as described at the crucifixion, also suffering the same pain Jesus would have felt.

Saint Francis garden statue. Photograph by Diane Browne copyright 2022.

Francis died on October 3, 1226, around the age of 45. His last two years had been one of constant pain and after contracting an eye disease, was almost blind.

Francis is one of the more popular saints in artwork and statues. He is often depicted with a bird in his hand which comes from a story during a journey with fellow friars. When they came upon some trees filled with birds, Francis stopped and began preaching to them. The birds sat on the branches listening, with not one flying away until he told them they may go.

Only two years after his death, on

July 16, 1228, Pope Gregory IX declared Francis a saint. He was given the feast day of October 4, becoming the patron saint of animals.

Francis was awarded further honors when Pope Pius XII jointly named Francis of Assisi and Catherine of Siena patron saints of Italy on June 18, 1938. Then on November 29, 1979, Pope John Paul II declared Francis a patron saint of ecology.

Four years after his death on May 25, 1230, Francis was interred in the Lower Balisica, which was built to suit the Franciscan Order in one way and Francis in another. For a man who lived as he preached of poverty, he asked to be buried on the hillside known as Hell Hill below Assisi. For fear that the grave would be ransacked by invaders, it remained hidden until it was discovered in 1818. Between 1927 and 1930, an elaborate tomb fit for a king was built for Francis. But he wasn't allowed to rest, proving the reason for him to be hidden, when his remains were examined in 1978 and placed in a glass urn. The church and his tomb are now popular tourist attractions.

THE TWO TEACHERS

Charlotte Anne Moberly.

When "An Adventure" was published in 1911 by two ladies claiming to have travelled back in time, it soon became a best seller and much later, became known as the Moberly-Jourdain Incident. Charlotte Moberly and the younger Eleanor Jourdain wrote "An Adventure" under the pen names Elizabeth Morrison and Frances Lamont.

Charlotte Anne Elizabeth Moberly was born at Winchester on September 16, 1846. Her father, George Moberly, was a principal at Oxford University before becoming Archbishop of Salisbury in 1869. In 1886, Charlotte also became a principal at Oxford University, being one of the first females As she got older, it was decided that she needed an assistant to lighten her load, and Eleanor Jourdain applied for the post.

Eleanor Frances Jourdain was born at Derwent Woodland, Derbyshire, on November 16, 1863. She was the oldest of ten children to Francis Jourdain, a vicar of Ashbourne, Derbyshire. The family wasn't wealthy and her grandparents financed her education at Oxford. Her first job was secretary to the Archbishop of Canterbury before being put forward for the post of Charlotte Moberly's assistant.

Neither of the ladies married, and both were published writers before and after "An Adventure." It took ten years of research before deciding to publish their individual experiences during a day out. They both knew it would be hard for others, especially their peers, to believe that there could be no more than a reasonable explanation. Using pseudonyms to avoid ridicule, it's doubtful that they thought the book would become so popular to be a bestseller with several reprints.

Charlotte Moberly, wishing to have a friendly association with her new assistant, looked at spending some time with Eleanor Jourdain. Miss Jourdain was teaching English children living in Paris and having an apartment in the city, invited Charlotte to stay with her. They arranged to visit several places in the area and on August 10, 1901, Miss Moberly (54) and Miss Jourdain (37) took a train to Versailles, where they toured the palace. Not being overly impressed and having plenty of time before catching the train, they decided to take a walk in the Pettit Trianon Gardens. Using a Baedeker guidebook, the ladies believed they missed the turning that would have taken them onto the main avenue and soon became lost.

It was on taking a woodland footpath that an oppressive atmosphere came over them, though at the time, neither mentioned it. Charlotte wondered why Eleanor didn't ask for directions from a woman shaking a sheet out of the window of a house. Then they came upon what they thought were gardeners has there was a wheelbarrow nearby, and asking directions, were told to go straight on. At this point, Eleanor Jourdain saw what looked to be a farmer's cottage, where a young girl and woman stood in the doorway. Miss Jourdain remembered thinking how old fashioned their clothes looked. Following the path, as directed, they saw a building like a bandstand which the ladies called a kiosk. The area appeared to be deserted with no other tourists. Both women felt some trepidation on seeing a man sitting close to the kiosk who gave the impression of being a sinister character that neither wanted to approach. At this point, the path had two options, either going left and passing the man or turning right. However, the decision was made for them when a young man, seeming to come from nowhere, ran up to them and in French told them to go right. Waving his hand in a sweeping gesture towards the path, he told them to look for the house. He then ran on, and when the ladies turned to thank him, although they could hear the sound of running feet, he was nowhere to be seen. For some reason, they felt that he had an assignation with the other man and wanted them out of the way before beginning a duel, this seeming to be a vivid imagination.

The path took them to a bridge crossing a ravine that they continued to follow to a canopy of trees. The footpath took them to the English Garden of a smaller house than the ladies expected. It was here that Charlotte saw a lady on a camp stool who appeared to be sketching the trees. Passing close by, the woman raised her head to look at them, but didn't speak, as neither did they, with Charlotte thinking her dress was unusually old fashioned. In her description, Charlotte said she looked away, feeling annoyed by the woman's presence.

Continuing to the terrace at the north side of the house, they found the windows boarded up. Charlotte saw the sketching lady walking along the terrace and was pleased that Eleanor hadn't asked her if the house was open. Walking around the house to look for an entrance, a door was suddenly flung open and a young man came out, slamming it shut behind him. Seeing the two teachers, he called

Marie Antoinette

to them, telling them the way into the house was by the courtyard. As he obligingly escorted them around the outside of the house, the ladies got the impression that he was a footman, though he wasn't in uniform.

Going through the door into the house, they found themselves alone in the entrance hall until a wedding party arrived. Falling in step with the procession, they moved from one room to another. Though the tour around the Petit Trianon was interesting, being at the back of the group meant they could hardly hear the guide's narrative of the history. On exiting, a small carriage was waiting in the courtyard that took them to the Hotel des Reservoirs in Versailles, where they had tea before taking the train back to Paris.

Lying 12-miles outside of Paris, the history of the Palace of Versailles is a long one. Originally it was a hunting lodge used by Louis XIII, who replaced it with a small chateau. Over the years, there have been many changes to its scenery. Louis XIV expanded the chateau for it to become a palace, converting the swampy land into magnificent parkland and gardens. It became the main-residence when the court and government were transferred from Paris. Louis XV spent a happy childhood at the palace, but under the regency of his mother, the court returned to the capital. Little work was carried out under Louis XV or Louis XVI, with European wars and crop failures draining France's wealth. Louis XVI and Marie Antoinette were married at Versailles, and all four of their children were born there.

The palace has been the scene of some historical events. The American War of Independence was concluded with France and Spain signing separate treaties with Britain at Versailles. The French Revolution began due to changes made at Versailles by the government to appease certain factions. Like the revolt in Russia that occurred 128-years later, the women of France, who had no political leanings, went on a march to protest against the limited supply of food and high prices. When men joined the fray, it took them from Paris to Versailles.

The Petit Trianon was built by Louis XV for his mistress, Jeanne Antoinette Poisson, better known as Madame de Pompadour, and was later given to Marie Antoinette. Marie Antoinette was seen as a foreigner by the French, but more so an Austrian who had at one time been their enemy. Many malicious rumors circulated about Marie Antoinette, mostly unfounded, from being a thief to an immoral woman. It was widely believed that her only surviving son and heir to the French throne was fathered by one of her many lovers. To excuse the revolution and the debts caused by its wars, the French people laid total blame on the shoulders of Marie Antoinette.

When Napoleon Bonaparte became the French Emperor, he looked at making the Palace of Versailles one of his main-residences. By this time, it had fallen into disuse and being careful not to be accused of opulence like the royal family, Bonaparte decided to restore the Grand Trianon, which he used as a spring retreat.

The Palace was later turned into a museum, its artwork and statues having long been taken to the Louvre in Paris. Today, Versailles is one of the worlds most visited tourist attractions.

Over the next few days, Charlotte and Eleanor visited other sites, including the tombs of Louis XVI and Marie Antoinette at Saint-Denis, being pleasant outings. Neither talked of their trip to Versailles or the unusually dressed people they saw on the way. They didn't know one another well enough to talk about how they felt. Of the oppressive atmosphere, the feelings of anxiety, and the underlying fear of the man seated by the kiosk, which continued to affect them both.

The visit to Versailles continued to weigh on the minds of the two women. Charlotte especially, as writing a letter to her friend relating their visit, had to put down her pen as that same oppression came over her. She finally asked Eleanor Jourdain if she thought the Petit Trianon was haunted, to which she replied, "Yes."

The visit over, Charlotte Moberly returned to England. It wasn't until November that Miss Jourdain went to stay with Charlotte. Neither could forget the visit to Versailles, but it wasn't until their last evening that the subject came up. When Miss Moberly mentioned the lady sat sketching and how they could have asked her for directions to enter the house, Miss Jourdain showed surprise. She had not seen any lady, even though she was looking for someone to ask.

It was decided that they would write an account of their experience and what they saw from realizing they were lost. Miss Jourdain left the next morning and two days later, Miss Moberly received Eleanor's recollections.

They both listed the gardeners who had given them directions, describing their clothes as green, which matched. However, Miss Moberly didn't see the farmhouse, the girl or the woman.

They both saw and heard the running man, and both felt ill at ease on seeing the man seated by the kiosk, describing him as having darkish skin and a scarred face of pockmarks.

Instead of leaving it as a mystery to relate to family and friends, the two teachers began to research the history. They didn't know what happened that day, but felt the need to find out if the people they had seen were simply actors reenacting the past or if it was something more paranormal.

Eleanor Frances Jourdain.

Eleanor Jourdain returned to Versailles on a wet day in January the following year. This time she took a different path, but when she came to the bridge those same feelings of oppression returned. On this second visit, the trees were more spacious, the leaves having fallen with it being winter. She saw two men collecting sticks and putting them into a cart.

With the thought that she could ask them for directions if she got lost, she went on a little farther. Turning to look back, she could see where the men had been, but in only a few minutes had disappeared, cart and all. As in August, she felt, rather than saw people on the path, with what she interpreted as a rustling of silk, and heard a voice call out in French, "Sir and Madam." Then there was the sound of a band, as though the music was coming in waves on the wind.

Miss Jourdain asked if a band had been playing that day but was told they usually would play every Thursday but had played the day before on New Year's Day.

Telling friends of the second visit, Miss Jourdain learned that the ghost of Marie Antoinette had often been seen making butter in the dairy. That was where the queen was when a page ran to her with a message telling her a mob marching from Paris would be at the gates within the hour.

Charlotte and Eleanor turned their attention to the people they had seen. They learned that the gardeners never wore green, as the color was reserved for the royal livery. They found that a family lived in a house that Miss Jourdain described, having had a daughter named Marion.

In their research, they procured a couple of maps from around 1840, showing a round building in the area of the kiosk. They came up with the theory that the man sitting by the kiosk could have been the Comte de Vaudreuil, a favorite of Marie Antoinette, with the rumor that they had an affair. The running man was put down as being the messenger who informed the queen that the mob was on its way.

Charlotte and Eleanor believed or wanted to believe that they had gone back in time, to October 5, 1789. But this is only a conjecture with the ladies attempting to fit their unusual walk into a time that would fit in with their experiences.

On seeing a portrait of Marie Antoinette, Miss Moberly was more certain than ever that she had seen the queen sketching in the garden at the Petit Trianon.

In their research, they collected any books they found that gave a history of Marie Antoinette and the houses and grounds of the palace.

Making several more visits to Versailles 10-years later, they felt ready to publish "An Adventure," which is still in print, online at Project Gutenberg and available as an audiobook.

After years of speculation as to the identity of the authors, it wasn't revealed until the late 1920s, when Charlotte Moberly was in her eighties. Though retired, she was still on the governing council at Oxford.

On the other hand, Eleanor Jourdain had become a principal at Oxford. Wanting things done her way, in November 1923, she approached the council accusing a tutor, Cecilia Mary Ady, of undermining her authority and insisting she be dismissed. Before this, the two ladies had been friends and fellow activists. Ady, who was popular and well written, objected to the sacking, which many believed was pure jealousy on Eleanor Jourdain's part. When Cecilia received support from fellow tutors and council members who resigned and held boycotts, it caught the attention of the newspapers. An investigation was instigated, which exonerated Cecilia of all wrongdoing. Eleanor Jourdain would have received a request to resign, but avoided the embarrassment by dying on April 6, 1924. Her death left Charlotte Moberly to defend the story as being a true account.

THE UNSOLVED MURDERS

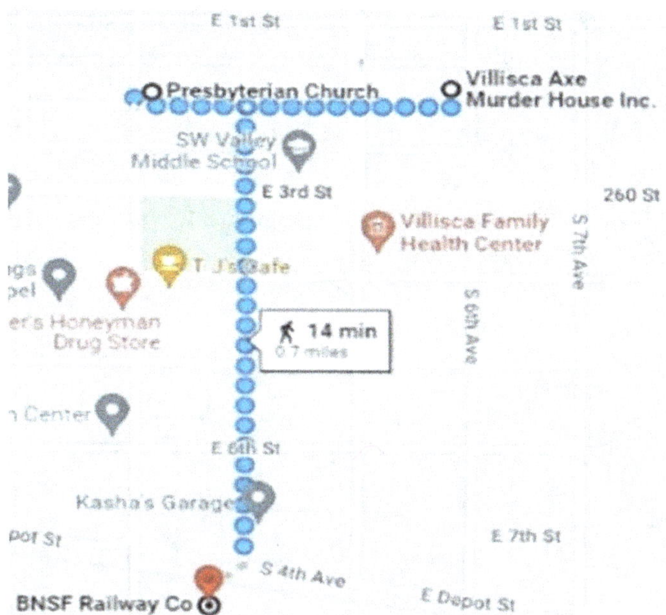

Routes from Presbyterian Church, Moore's house and
train station. Map date copyright 2022 Google.

One of the most gruesome murders in Iowa saw two adults and six children killed with an axe. The murderer got away, leaving the mystery of their identity to this day.

The Villisca murders have never gained as much attention as the axe murder of two people in Falls River, Massachusetts, 24-years earlier. Maybe because it was a female accused of the crime as Lizzie Borden was charged even though there were other suspects. It may well have helped get her acquitted, apart from the prosecution presenting nothing more than theories.

On Sunday, June 9, 1912, Mr. Josiah "Joe" Moore, his wife Sara and their four children, Herman Montgomery (11), Mary Catherine (10), Arthur Boyd (7), and Paul Vernon (5), attended the Presbyterian Church. Sara Moore had helped to organize the Children's Day

Service in which her children took part. Two friends of Mary, Lena Gertrude Stillinger (11) and Ina May Stillinger (8), also took part and were invited to stay the night at the Moore house. The Stillinger girls lived two and a half miles out of town, and Joe Moore telephoned their home and spoke to Blanche Stillinger, their older sister, to ask if the girls could stay the night. It was probably a welcome invitation as their mother, Sarah Stillinger, was 7-months pregnant with her seventh child. The baby boy only lived two days and is interred beside his sisters.

After the service, the Moore's remained to prepare bouquets of flowers for the sick. The last to leave the church was Reverend Wesley Ewing, his wife and a visiting preacher, Reverend George Jacklin Kelly, who had arrived that morning.

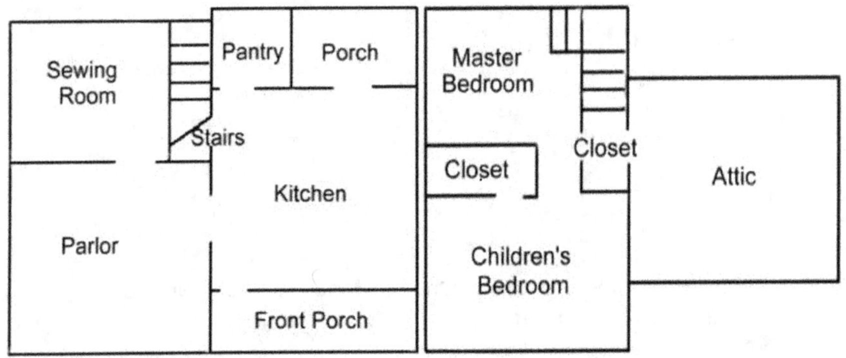

Moore's house lower floor.   Moore's house upper floor.

At 9.30pm, Mr. and Mrs. Moore, their children and two young guests walked to the house, arriving no later than 10.00pm. Two young men, Orville and Floyd Watts, walked with the Moore's to their home on what was a dark night as the street lights weren't working due to a dispute with the power company, leaving only a slit of a waning moon. They saw Joe take a key from his pocket and unlock the front door. Being the last people to see them alive, they claimed that one of the girls said she could see a man in the trees. There were hobos around the town who were told to leave by the Marshall, and they took a train going to Creston.

Apart from the basement only having access from outside, the ground floor has a covered porch to the front and rear doors. Lena and

Ina shared a bed in the guest room on the first floor, while Joe and Sara had their own room directly from the top of the stairs, which today would be called open-plan. Off Sara and Joe's bedroom is a closet, which at the time was covered by a sheet but at the back is a door leading to an attic room used for storage. The attic has two eerie windows on a smaller scale to the ones which had once been a feature of the Amityville Horror House. Another door from the parents' bedroom led to the children's room, where all four Moore children slept.

No one knows the exact time the murders took place. It's believed that when the family returned from church, someone was already in the house. Someone who had taken a long-handled axe from Joe's shed and sat in the attic room waiting for everyone to go to bed and fall asleep. Sneaking out of the attic room, the murderer stood looking down at a sleeping Joe and Sara. Swinging the axe, they were struck on the head. In the children's room, all four were hit on the head with the flat end of the axe. Then it was downstairs to Lena and Ina, who had been so excited about staying overnight with their friends. As a final insult, Lena's nightdress was pulled up, and there were bloodstains on her arm and a leg as she was positioned on the bed.

Returning to the bedroom of Joe and Sara for another attack, the axe was wielded so violently that it struck the wall and low ceiling. If the axe had struck the ceiling in the initial killing, it would have woken the household. Either before or after the killings, the curtains were drawn at each window, and one without curtains had a sheet pinned to it. The doors, windows and mirrors were covered with torn clothing, leaving numerous theories as to why the killer would not want to see a reflection of themselves. A sheet was pulled over Joe and Sara, and all the children had clothes covering their heads.

Being bathed in blood, the murderer having covered all the windows would make a low-lit lamp harder to see from outside, allowing time to wash. Being so carefully planned, the murderer no doubt would have had clean clothes to change into.

Finding a slab of bacon, this was left on the floor beside the Stillinger girls with the axe. As there was plenty of time before the crime would be discovered, the killer prepared and ate a meal. They then left the house, locking the door and taking the keys. Nothing else was known to be missing, being a case of murder rather than theft if the food and keys aren't taken into account.

The house has now been restored to how it was in 1912, becoming a tourist attraction claiming to be one of the most haunted houses in America.

The following morning, the Moore's neighbor, Mary Peckham, noticed how quiet the house was. By 7am, when there was no sign of anyone coming out to feed the chickens, she knocked on the door and, with no reply, found it to be locked. She then called Joe's brother, Ross and spoke to his wife, Jesse, to ask if anything had happened to Joe's father, knowing that Charles Moore was ill. Jesse called Ross at work, and he shortly arrived at the house with spare keys.

Looking around the downstairs, he found Lena and Ina and told Mary Peckham to call Hank Horton, the town's peace officer. When Horton arrived, he searched the upstairs to discover that the whole family had been murdered.

Cigarette butts found in the attic room were put down as clues that one or two people had been waiting there until the household was asleep. Many people streamed through the small house, contaminating what little forensic evidence would have been available during that era.

Over the next several weeks, any strangers or transients in the area were rounded up and interrogated. Family, friends, neighbors and Joe's business contacts were all questioned. There were numerous suspects with grievances against Joe Moore, but not to the point that it would call for someone to kill the whole family.

The visiting Reverend George Kelly had left town early on Monday morning before the alarm was raised. He was thought to take an unusual interest in the murders, arousing suspicion by writing to the police and investigators on the case. It didn't help that he had mental problems during his teenage years and had been caught peeping through house windows. When looking for a secretary to type a manuscript he claimed to be writing, he put an advert in a newspaper. During the job interview he stipulated that they must type in the nude.

He took the 5.19am train to go home to his wife, Laura and during the journey, told an elderly couple of the murders, which hadn't yet been discovered. Once he got away from Villisca, he sent a shirt with blood on it to be cleaned.

It wasn't until 1917 that he was arrested and admitted to committing the crime. When it came to his trial, charged with only murdering Lena Stillinger, he recanted. The jury was split, leading to a hung jury. In a second trial, he was acquitted.

At the time, some thought the Villisca case was linked to other similar murders. There was an axe murder at Colorado Springs before Villisca. Beautiful 25-year-old Alice May Burnham was looking after her two children, Nellie (7) and John (2). as her husband, Arthur Burnham (40), was a resident at the Modern Woodman Sanatorium.

Alison and the children were asleep when someone entered their home and killed all three with an axe. They were found on September 20, 1911, but had died days before, being put down to Sunday the 17th. Arthur was quickly dropped as a suspect and died five months later from Bright's Disease and Tuberculosis.

It wasn't the only murder that night. Francis Henry Wayne (24), Blanche Vera Wayne (23) and their daughter Lulu May Wayne (2) moved to Colorado and, within days, were dead. The move was to get medical help for Henry Wayne at the Modern Woodman Sanatorium, though, unlike his neighbor, John Burnham, he was at home. Like the Villisca murders, it was a Sunday night when the murderer entered the houses on Hurricane Place, the Wayne's, and West Dale Street, the Burnham's. The killer had covered the bodies and left the axe by the back door of the Wayne's house.

One month later, at Ellsworth, Kansas, someone entered the two-room cottage of the Showman family. On Sunday, October 15, 1911, William Showman (31), his wife Pauline (27), their children Lester (6), Fern (4) and Fenton (19 months) visited the Snook family, leaving for the short walk home at around 9.00pm.

The axe used to kill the family was left at the property, and those working on the case believed it was someone known to them as their dog didn't raise the alarm. Instead, it was put outside and went to the Snook's several times during the day, yet, it was found in the house when the bodies were discovered later that evening.

Bloodhounds followed a trail that was lost when they reached the railroad crossing. A bloodstained shirt was found in a hotel room, but no one could say who the man renting it was as he had used it for no more than a couple of hours.

Due to the belief that it was someone who knew the Showman's because of the dog, the main suspect was Charles Marzyck. He had done jail time for theft and was divorced from William's sister. It was said there was bad blood, with Marzyck threatening to kill his former wife and the Showman's. Marzyck was charged, but producing a cast-iron alibi, the judge threw the case out of court.

A sketch was made of the man who booked the hotel room, bearing a similar resemblance to Charles Marzyck, but also a likeness to Reverend George Kelly.

Charles Marzyck. Police booking Photo.

Police sketch of man who booked room at Baker Hotel.

Reverend George Kelly. Photo credit Villisca Living with a Mystery.

Unless any evidence collected remains, such as fingerprints that could be matched, these murders will remain unsolved.

WEBSITE REFERENCES

AL CAPONE
Atlas Obscurer
Article: Al Capone Cherry Tree,
Baltimore, Maryland.
atlasobscurer.com

History Collection
Many articles on Al Capone
historycollection.com

Houstonia Magazine
Article: In Chicago and Beyond, Hunting
the Ghost of Al Capone by Bill Wiatrak.
houstoniamagazine.com

The Mob Museum
300 Stewart Avenue, Las Vegas,
NV 89101
Open to the public.
themobmuseum.org

Al Capone Museum
owned by Mario Gomez
myalcaponemuseum.com

ASSASSINATION & CURSE OF ABRAHAM LINCOLN
Ford's Theater
514 Tenth Street, Washington DC 20004.
The assassination, history of the Theater
and the Peterson House.
ford.org

Library of America
Articles and Speeches and Writings.
loa.org

Library of Congress
Articles & Photographs
loc.gov

Spartacus Educational
Pictures: Abraham Lincoln, David Herold,
Lewis Powell & George Atzerodt
spartacus-educational.com

White House History
Article: Seances in the Red Room
whitehousehistory.com

THE BELL WITCH
The Bell Witch
Article: Bell Witch lore spins dark tale,
but could science explain it all? by Katie
Nixon
eu.tennessee.com

The Bell Witch Site
owned by Pat Fitzhugh
bellwitch.org

The Official Home of the Bell Witch Cave
430 Keyberg Road, Adams TN 37010
Open by appointment
bellwitchcave.com

Youtube
Documentary: 200 Year Old
Tennessee Haunting – Bogeymen – The
Bell Witch
youtube.com

BLACK AGGIE
Dying To Tell Their Stories
Article: Black Aggie: The urban
legend that won't die
dyingtotelltheirstories.com

Fat Tire Tours
Article: History Lesson Black Aggie
fattiretours.com

Odd Things I've Seen
owned by J. W. Ocker, award
winning author
Article: The Black Aggie
oddthingsiveseen.com

BLUFF CREEK BIGFOOT
CBC Radio
Transcript of interview: Cowboy
behind legendary Patterson-Gimlin
Bigfoot film marks 50th anniversary
cbc.ca

Smithsonian Magazine
Article: Why Do So Many People Still
Want to Believe in Bigfoot? by Ben Crair
smithsonianmag.com

WEBSITE REFERENCES

Wikipedia-Rick Dyer (hoaxer)
wikipedia.org

THE COTTINGLEY FAIRIES
Historic UK
Article: The Cottingley Fairies by Miriam Bibby
historic-uk.com

Museum of Hoaxes
Article: The Cottingley Fairies
hoaxes.org

On : Yorkshire Magazine
Article: The Cottingley Fairies: An Innocent Hoax by Matt Callard
on-magazine.co.uk

Science Media Museum
Pictureville, Bradford BD1 1NQ
Open to the public
scienceandmediamuseum.org.uk

THE CURSED CAR
HGM Krieg Museum of Military History
Article: Sarajevo Assassination June 28, 1914.
Arsenal 1, 1030 Wien, Austria
Open to the public
hgm.at

Hidden Histories WWI
Article: November 1913: The Archduke, Nottingham and a Near Miss by Michael Noble
hiddenhistorieswwi.ac.uk

Smithsonian Magazine
Article: Curses! Archduke Franz Ferdinand and His Astounding Death Car by Mike Dash
smithsoniammag.com

THE CURSED FILM SCRIPT
IMDB John Belushi
imdb.com/name/nm0000004

IMDB John Candy

imdb.com/name/nm000106

IMDB Chris Farley
imdb.com/name/nm0000394

IMDB Sam Kinison
imdb.com/name/nm000106

Screen Play Movie Blogspot
Article: Atuk
screenplaymovie.blogspot.com

Wikipedia
Article: The Incomparable Atuk
wikipedia.com

CRYBABY BRIDGES
Atlas Obscura
Article: Van Sant Crybaby Bridge
atlasobscura.com

Ohio Exploration Society
Exploring locations in Ohio
ohioexploration.com

Only In Your State
Article: The Oklahoma Legend Will Send Chills Down Your Spine by Catherine Armstrong
onlyinyourstate.com

DR CRIPPEN – AN INNOCEDNT MAN!
The History Press
Article: The Notorious Case of Dr Crippen
thehistorypress.co.uk

Mirror Newspaper
Article: The secret life of Victorian killer: Dr Crippen's mistress revealed 107 years ago after wife's murder by Laura Connor
mirror,co.uk

Murderpedia
owned by Juan Ignacio Blanco
Article: Dr Hawley Harvey Crippen
murderpedia.org

The Oldie

WEBSITE REFERENCES

Article: Mutilating the Evidence by Bob Woffinden
theoldie.co.uk

The Proceedings of the Old Bailey
Trial Transcript: Hawley Harvey Crippen
Trial Transcript: Ethel Clara Le Neve
oldbaileyonline.org

UCR Center for Bibliographical Studies and Research
Newspaper: Los Angeles Herald
November 13, 1910
cbsr.ucr.edu

THE ENFIELD POLTERGEIST
BBC
BBC4 The Reunion
bbc.co.uk

Enfield Independent
Article: "They were terrified." The men who saw the Enfield poltergeist petrify an entire family
enfieldindependent.co.uk

THE FLORIDA SKUNK APE
Skunk Ape Headquarters
40904 Tamiami Trail, East Ochopee FL 34141
Open to the public
paradisecoast.com

Shealys Official Skunkape Headquarters
skunkape.info

Smithsonian Magazine
Article: On The Trail of Florida's Bigfoot – the Skunk Ape by Joseph Stromberg
smithsonianmag.com

FORETELLING OF THE TITANIC
History
Article: Titanic
history.com

Project Gutenberg
Book: The Wreck of the Titan original title

Futility by Morgan Robertson
gutenberg.org

Syracuse com
Article: Central NY News-The strange tale of an Oswego man who wrote a book predicting a Titanic-like disaster… 14 years before it happened by Debra J Groom. The Post Standard
syracuse.com

Titanic Belfast
Titanic Exhibition
1 Olympic Way, Belfast, N Ireland BT3 9
Open to the public
titanicbelfast.com

W. T. Stead Resource Site
Official website of Victorian newspaper editor, William Thomas Stead
attackingthedevil.co.uk

THE MARY CELESTE
Lost at Sea Memorials
Article: Mary Celeste Memorial – Spencer's Island, Nova Scotia
lost-at-sea-memorials.com

Slate
Article: Ghost Ship by Paul Collins
slate.com

Smithsonian Magazine
Article: Abandoned Ship: The Mary Celeste by Jess Blumberg
smithsonianmag.com

MERMAIDS
Durham World Heritage Site
Article: The Norman Chapel
durhamworldheritagesite.com

Exemplore
Article: Mermaid Sightings and Speculation by Suzette Horspool
exemplore.com

Guinness World Records
Article: Stunning underwater

WEBSITE REFERENCES

mermaid show breaks record in China by Echo Zhan
guinnessworldrecords.com

History
This Day in History: 01/09/1493
Christopher Columbus Sees Mermaids
history.com

Live Science
Article: Mermaid Sightings Claimed in Israel by Benjamin Radford
livescience.com

Live Science
Article: Mermaids and Mermen – Facts and Legends by Benjamin Radford and Scott Dutfield
livescience.com

Museum of Hoaxes
Article: The Feejee Mermaid
hoaxes.org

Scandification
Article: Denmarks Little Mermaid: 25 things you should know about the story and statue
scandification.com

Strange History
Article: Caithness Mermaid Mystery? by Beach Combing
strangehistory.net

THE POOKA
Connolly Cove
Article: Digging into the secrets of Irish Pookas
connollycove.com

Emerald Isle
Article: The Pooka
emeraldisle.ie

Irish Central
Article: The Irish Legend of the Pooka by Leo Casey

irishcentral.com

Project Gutenberg
Short Story: The Kildare Pooka by Patrick Kennedy published 1866
gutenberg.org

QUEEN ANNE'S STATUE
Rick May
Article: Queen Anne in Hastings
rickmay.co.uk

Wikipedia
Article: Statue of Queen Anne, Queen Anne's Gate
wikipedia.org

ST. FRANCIS OF ASSISI
Biography
Article: Saint Francis of Assisi
biography.com

Church Pop
Article: The Mystery of the Hidden Tomb of St Francis of Assisi
churchpop.com

Franciscan Media
Article: A Franciscan on the Stigmata of St Francis by Jack Wintz O.F.X
franciscanmedia.org

The Humane Society of the United States
Article: St Francis of Assisi
humanesociety.org

THE TWO TEACHERS
Academic Dictionaries and Encyclopedias
Article: Moberly-Jourdain Incident
academic.com

Hub Pages
Article: Time Slip- Anne Moberly and Eleanor Jourdain – The Ghost of Versailles
discover.hubpages.com

WEBSITE REFERENCES

Project Gutenberg
Book: An Adventure by Eleanor F
Jourdain and C.A.E Moberly
published by MacMillan and Co.
Limited
gutenberg.org

Wikipedia
Article: Charlotte Anne Moberly
wikipedia.org

Wikipedia
Article: Eleanor Jourdain
wikipedia.org

THE UNSOLVED MURDERS
Genealogy Trails
Article: Barnham/Wayne Killings
genealogytrails.com

Google Maps
googlemaps.com

Historic Mysteries
Article: Unsolved Villisca Axe Murders of
1912 by Joe Turner
historicmysteries.com

Kansas Trails
Article: Ellsworth County, Kansas
genealogytrails.com

Smithsonian Magazine
Article: The Ax Murderer Who Got Away
by Mike Dash
smithsonianmag.com

Villisca Ax Murder House
508 E 2nd Street, Villisca, Iowa 50864
Open to the public
villiscaiowa.com

BOOK REFERENCES

AL CAPONE
Al Capone : The Life, Legacy and Legend *by Deirdre Blair*
Anchor Books

Get Capone: The Secret Plot That Captured America's Most Wanted Gangster *by Jonathan Eig*
Simon and Schuster

Uncle Al Capone *by Deirdre Marie Capone*
Recaplodge LLC
Author website unclealcapone.com

THE ASSASSINATION & CURSE OF ABRAHAM LINCOLN
Booth and His Assassins, Lincoln and His Avengers *by Dr William W. Joyce*
CreateSpace Independent Publishing

Lewis Thornton Powell – The Conspiracy to Kill Abraham Lincoln *by Sydney St. James*
Beebop Publishing Group

Lincoln's Assassination *by Edward Steers Jr.*
Southern Illinois University Press

THE BELL WITCH
History of the Famous Bell Witch *by M. V. Ingram*
Independently Published

The Bell Witch – An American Haunting *by Brent Monahan*
St. Martin's Press

BLUFF CREEK BIGFOOT
The Bigfoot Book: The Encyclopedia of Sasquatch, Yeti and Cryptid Primates (The Real Unexplained Collection) *by Nick Redfern*
Visible Ink

The Bluff Creek Project: The Patterson-Gimlin Bigfoot Film Site A

Journey of Rediscovery *by Robert Letterman*
Independently Published

THE COTTINGLEY FAIRIES
The Coming of the Fairies – The Cottingley Incident *by Sir Arthur Conan Doyle*
CreateSpace Independent Publishing

Sir Arthur Conan Doyle and The Secret of the Cottingley Fairies *by F. R. Maher*
Independently Published

THE CURSED CAR
Archduke Franz Ferdinand and the Era of Assassination *by Lisa Traynor*
Trustees of the Royal Armories

One Morning in Sarajevo *by David James Smith*
W & M Publishing

THE CURSED FILM SCRIPT
The Incomparable Atuk *by Mordecai Richler*
Andre Deutsch Publishing 1st edition

DR CRIPPEN – AN INNOCENT MAN!
Mr. Crippen, Cora and the Body in the Basement *by Matthew Coniam*
Pen & Sword True Crime

Walter Dew – The Man Who Caught Crippen *by Nicholas Connell*
The History Press

THE ENFIELD POLTERGEIST
The Enfield Poltergeist Tapes – One of the most disturbing cases in history, What Really Happened? *by Melvyn J. Willin*
White Crow Books

This House is Haunted – The True Story of the Enfield Poltergeist *by Guy Lyon Playfair*
White Crow Books

BOOK REFERENCES

THE FLORIDA SKUNK APE
The Florida Keys Skunk Ape Files *by Brad Bertolli*
Independently Published

Skunk Ape – Florida's Bigfoot *by George Dunning*
Independently Published

FORETELLING OF THE TITANIC
Titanic on Trial – The Night the Titanic Sunk *by Nic Compton*
Adlard Coles Publishers

Titanic's Last Secret *by John Hamer*
CreativeSpace Independent Publishing

W. T. Stead and the Conspiracy of 1910 to Save The World *by Robert Livingston*
Book Trail Publishing

Wreck of the Titan or Futility *by Morgan Robertson*
CreateSpace Independent Publishing

THE MARY CELESTE
Ghost Ship – The Mysterious True Story of the Mary Celeste and Her Missing Crew *by Brian Hicks*
Random House Inc.

MERMAIDS
Among the Mermaids: Facts, Myths and Enchantments from the Sirens of the Sea *by Varla Ventura*
Red Wheel/Weiser Publications

THE POOKA
Fairies, Pookas and Changelings : A Complete Guide to the Wild and Wicked Enchanted Realm *by Varla Venturer*
Red Wheel/Weiser Publications

ST. FRANCIS OF ASSISI
St Francis of Assisi *by G. K. Chesterton*
Independently Published

The Writing of St. Francis of Assisi
CreativeSpace Independent Publishing

THE TWO TEACHERS
An Adventure *by C. A. Moberly & E. F. Jourdain*
Martino Fine Books

THE UNSOLVED MURDERS
Fiend Incarnate : Villisca Axe Murders of 1912 *by Edgar V. Epperly*
Independently Published

A Nightmare in Villisca : Investigating the Haunted Axe Murder House *by Richard Estep*
Independently Published

BIOGRAPHY

Diane Browne lives in Nottinghamshire, England, with her cats and a grumpy old man she calls Dad.

She is a honored poet and has had short stories published in magazines. This is her fifth book, the first, "5 Paranormal Tales" begins a series of "5 Tales" of five short stories. Added to this is "5 More Paranormal Tales" and "5 Tudor Tales." There is also a movie script gathering dust somewhere in Los Angeles.

She fell into radio in 2005 when Kirk Haskell aka "DJ Captain Kirk," asked her to volunteer her services on his radio station, "Heartbeat of Flagler" based in Florida. Diane moderated the chat room, produced adverts and participated in phone-in segments.

In 2012 she produced and co-hosted "Weird News Weekly" with Norman Soldwish Jr, in Ohio. The show became syndicated, playing on several internet stations. Having family commitments, Diane and Norm had less time to devote to the hours that went into every show, the last airing in 2019. She also joined the team at her local hospital radio station, Trust AM and is back on air presenting local news, though her radio show is presently on hiatus.

At the beginning of 2022, Diane published her first novel, "Victor's Place," set in New York during the prohibition era.